TAO
THE WAY
OF THE
WAYS

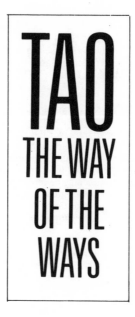

TAO
THE WAY
OF THE
WAYS

The Tao Te Ching

Translated and with a commentary

by Herrymon Maurer

Wildwood House

First published in Great Britain in 1986 by
Wildwood House Limited
Gower House, Croft Road
Aldershot, Hants GU11 3HR
England

Lao zu
Tao: the way of the ways
I. Title   II. Maurer, Herrymon   III. Dao de jing.
English
299'.51482   BL1900

ISBN 0-7045-0527-4

Printed in Great Britain at the
University Press, Cambridge

In Memoriam
Hu Shih
Chou Li-fei

CONTENTS

PART I: THE NOWNESS OF SCRIPTURE

PART II: THE TAO/VIRTUE CLASSIC

PRONUNCIATION KEY

Pronounce Lao as if it were the last syllable of allow.
Pronounce Tzŭ as if it were Dz, leaving off as much *u* as possible.

Pronounce Tao as if it were Dow.
Pronounce Teh as if it were Duh, but keep the *uh* brief.
Pronounce Ching as if it were the first syllable of jingle.

TAO
THE WAY
OF THE
WAYS

PART I

The Nowness of Scripture

1. The First Dropout

It has become obvious that conventional ways of living are culminating in a violence that, unless forsworn, can eliminate life itself. It has been assumed that knowledge of such danger is the best preventative of it. But danger grows, not because its consequences are unknown but because its inward roots are unrecognized. Whatever may be the origins of violence in general, today's violence is rooted in Western man's habit of persisting in himself, existing in himself, and relating to himself whatever happens. It is shown in his telling other people what to do and, failing response, of forcing them, trying to force them, or manipulating them. It is displayed in his practice of expressing *himself* in word and in action, in preference to expressing anything else to any other being. It is demonstrated more obviously in assaults in the streets, arson in the cities, threats and skirmishes among the nations. It is ultimately disclosed in preparations for Armageddon, for which terminal event, the nations, imbued with notions of self-defense and fears of aggression, devise the elimination of vast numbers if not the whole of mankind. The plan is to prevent wars against people. But the too likely consequence is eliminating the people.

But it may well be that people — people counted by the head to the number of billions — are likely to be annihilated not in spite of themselves but because of their selves. It may be that life-obliterating war is the cultural choice of men, women, and children whose inward violence (even if expressed in nothing more than contentiousness at home and competitiveness at work: or, conversely, self-anger and inadequacy at both places) creates the emotional soil for national and international plagues. Certainly, it is unlikely that there will be peace abroad until it is made welcome at home.

For even the opposition to violence is filled with violence: the violence of people of apparent good will who know no other way of life than doing their own thing and telling other people what to do. Among such people the inward symptoms of violence often multiply: the confusion, frustration, fear, guilt, self-hate, depression, loneliness, and like distempers of men and women who are at the mercy of their unconscious minds, trained for centuries in the contentious ways of convention. It is not that scientific discovery has outstripped spiritual growth, as so often stated, but that self has dispossessed spirit and confused even the common understanding of reality.

But there is another way: a way of experiencing reality and living in it. It is a way based on all of reality — all of a man's being and all of nature's workings — and not on a partial reality based on self-willed urges to overcome other people and conquer nature. It is a way to overcome violence, socially and personally. Perhaps it can be called *the* other way, for the ways that work against violence are all the same way.

> Something there is, without form and complete,
> Born between heaven and earth.
> Solitary and vast,
> Standing alone without change,
> Everywhere pervading all things,
> Mothering all beneath heaven.
> I don't know its name;
> I style it Tao,
> And for want of a name call it great.

This one way is traced in many and diverse scriptures. It is the word as it came to Moses, to Gautama, to Isaiah, to Mohammed, to Jesus, and to many other prophets who have found the Ultimate and have sought words to describe their finding. Their way is actually not so difficult to follow as it is hard to locate. It is not now a topic of general conversation, and there are few literary and scholarly productions in which to read about it, although conventional rationalizings abound.

Sometimes the scriptural sourceworks seem forbidding because they are claimed as possessions by people of moralistic self-will, if not of ill will and violent will. In recent times, inspired writings about Truth have been ratiocinated out of their actual meanings into monstrous conventionalisms of a so-called religious sort, embraced variously by militarists in Thailand when calling upon Buddha, by terrorist mullahs in Iran when seeking approval from the Qu'ran, by Argentine gangsters when rushing to the defense of torture, and by salvationist me-firsters throughout the world when claiming inerrant scriptural support for false righteousness, legalistic dogmatism, and suicidal national-statism. The new way of life to be found in the scriptures is to be found by an unconventional reading of them, that is, a prophetic and liberating reading, not a priestly, moralistic, and confining one. Obvious obstacles are doctrinaire veneration and self-serving misquotation.

Indeed, if Westerners are ever to let their own scriptures speak to them, it may be wise to try first to understand those of other places where false familiarity and pseudo-sanctity are less likely to be barriers. It is the venture of this book about Tao — literally, the *Way* — to translate and comment on a Chinese scripture that can lead to a discovery of the same Way in scriptures nearer at hand. In the life of the writer, a similar venture with this same scripture, the primary work of the Taoist canon, led to his finding again the Jewish and Christian scriptures in which he was reared and in which, quite literally, he continues to have his being. If it be said that man is not to be inspired by scriptures foreign to his upbringing, that none but the natives are to be saved, and that God will not listen to all his children but only to those with a particular interpretation of particular parts of a particular scripture, then it is necessary for those who seek the will of Truth rather than their own to cry sacrilege, for the offense is against God and consists of an ultimate violence that denies his love for his children, his presence within them, and his converse with them.

As for Lao Tzŭ, an anti-conventional sage who sought peace by keeping himself hidden, he can be introduced succinctly as the first dropout:

> Whoever keeps to Tao
> Does not want to be full.
> Not full, he can practice
> Concealment instead of accomplishment.

For, twenty-five hundred years ago, an old man who distrusted princes, decried rituals, and disliked names dropped out of the empire of Chou and went into exile. He left behind a book of some five thousand characters, called for the last two thousand years the Tao Teh Ching — the Tao Virtue Classic — which is today as it has long been the great sensation of Asian literature and Asian scripture. He wrote with vividness, with starkness, with simplicity, not without humor, and with such force that his short work bred Taoism, shaped Buddhism, led to Ch'an and Zen meditation, created Chinese landscape painting, influenced profoundly not so much what was done in China as the manner in which it was done, and served as a guidebook for persons everywhere who look for the inward power that brings inward meaning and comfort. To Westerners the book is important not primarily because of its past effect in Asia but because of its potential effect in a Western world that has so obviously lost its way and is trying so desperately to find a new one. Tao is *the Way* in the sense of *the path;* and the Tao Teh Ching, which appeared in the early morning of historical time, describes one of a variety of paths through life that, to repeat, have always been the same Way.

The first fact about this particular Way is that the man who wrote about it had no name. Lao Tzŭ is a description rather than an appellation. It can mean *old philosopher* or *old sir,* but it can also mean *old child* or *old fellow.* Lao Tzŭ kept himself so well hidden that very little is known of him except what he wrote. His early biographer, Ssŭ-ma Ch'ien, records a few titles and a few places, chronicles a chronologically impossible meeting with Confucius, and has not more of substance to report than the following:

"He was a man indeed . . . . In the State of Chou, he was historian in charge of the secret archives . . . .

"Lao Tzŭ practiced Tao and virtue. His teaching was the concealment of self and not having names. He lived for a long time in the State of Chou, but forseeing its decay he departed and came to the frontier. The officer of the frontier was of the name Yin Hsi. He said, 'Sir, you are about to dropout. I urge you to write a book for me.'

"Lao Tzŭ then wrote a book of a first and second part, discussing Tao and virtue, and he wrote five thousand and some characters. Then he departed.

"No one knows where he died."

That is all. But that little could be still less without changing the impact of the book of Tao, which depends on its author *not* being known. Scholarly doubts have been expressed as to whether Lao Tzŭ lived when he is said to have lived and even whether he lived at all. But his non-existence or his existence at any time else would only dramatize his concealment of self and not having names. He is, in convention's eyes, scandalously against self.

He is also against the autocratic, the patriarchal, the hierarchic, the superstitious, the ritualistic, the oppressive, and the violent. Such opposition was indeed unconventional, but it was not in itself scandalous. The completeness of Lao Tzŭ's scandal was his dropping out of Chinese civilization to live among the barbarians. It was a scandal as great to the Chinese as Hosea's taking a whore to wife was to the Israelites or as Jesus dying the death of a criminal was to the Romans. It was an act of unsurpassable uncouthness, a topsy-turvying of civilization itself. As the Jews put down temple prostitutes and as the Romans put down subversives, so did the Chinese throughout their history put down the barbarians to the north and west of their country. Their moral weakness was the mark of Chinese superiority. Indeed, the flight of their old Sage to the people they despised remains an eternal symbol of the despicability of conventional success.

Martin Buber suggests that it is because of this despicability that Lao Tzŭ's teaching of following Tao and doing nothing can reach out in a living manner to Westerners as no other Asian teaching can reach out. "We have begun to learn," writes Buber, "that success is of no consequence. We have begun to doubt the significance of historical success, i.e. the validity of the man who sets an end for himself, carries this end into effect, accumulates the necessary means of power and succeeds with these means of power: the typical modern Western man. I say, we begin to doubt the content of existence of this man. And there we come in contact with . . . the teaching that genuine effecting is not interfering, not giving vent to power, but remaining within oneself . . . . With us this knowledge does not originate as wisdom but as foolishness . . . . But there where we stand or there where we shall soon stand, we shall directly touch the reality for which Lao Tzŭ spoke." (See note, page 105.)

> Does anyone want to take the world
> And act on it?
> I don't see how he can succeed.
> The world is a sacred vessel
> Not to be acted on.
> Whoever acts on it spoils it;
> Whoever grasps at it loses it.

For Lao Tzŭ speaks about the joy of following a way of life, not about the tension of acting on the world and chasing success or about winning a reputation and making a big splash. He writes about a meeting, a relationship with Tao, with nature, with other persons: not about obeying one or another set of precepts and persisting in them against all comers. He proposes an attitude toward life that is full of warmth and awe, and not a reaction against life that finds fault, assigns praise and blame, determines guilt, and passes judgment. He demonstrates an ever-new way of thinking that puts to work the entire being of man and not simply the isolated function of cogitation. He emphasizes the Tao-given capacity of this being to fit in with creation so long as he does not demand that creation fit in with him.

He does not simply castigate success and substitute for success castigation; he demonstrates an entirely different manner of being alive. Moreover, he promises, through the following of the Way, a deliverance from the torments of ego, from guilts and anxieties, from rages and deceits, from denials and depressions, and from the violence and aloneness that attend the failure of success:

> Therefore the sage
> Puts himself last,
> Finds himself first.
> Abandons his self,
> Preserves his self.
> Is it not because he has no self
> That he is able to realize his self?

For persons brought up on counsels of achievement and self-reliance, the possibility of self-abandonment seems at first as remote as it is unwanted. The pain that success-seeking inflicts on people is typically seen by them not as something they inflict on themselves but as something inflicted upon them by external circumstances, often in the form of other competing people. (Thus it is possible to self-inflict new pain to distract from old.) For persons brought up on praise and blame, giving up guilt seems like nothing less than the defeat of all law and order, since they see principles and precepts as the moral adornments of successful people, even though it is obvious that dedication to principle is characteristic of dictators and scoundrels of the sort who exist to punish those who differ from them. Indeed, a great demand of Western society, imposed alike by people of ill-will and good-will, is ideological purity, an inescapable consequence of trying to make self the center of the cosmos. To persons educated in the conventional Western manner, cogitation of the sterile sort practiced by social, scholarly, political, theological, and military dogmatists is generally held to be man's last best hope, since salvation — personal or social — is supposed to result from concepts that will control nature, society, other selves, and even one's own self. Self-will's basic urge is to control something.

The goals pursued by the will to control may be good in themselves, such as seeking peace and eliminating oppression. But so long as the conventional tools of power and will are used, so long is it impossible to achieve the goals sought. Probably, it is from the use of these conventional tools that wars and conflicts arise. The ineffectiveness of the peace movement throughout most of the twentieth century may well result from its attempt to be successful in a war against war. It has been effective only when it renounced conventional tools, as did Gandhi's non-violent campaigns in India, perhaps the only instances of effective group effort for peace in the century. Underlying the testimony of Gandhi is the same relationship to life that underlies the book of Tao: a deep prophetic awareness of the power of the spiritual reality that undergirds all life, together with a realization that this power can produce tremendous changes in society that cannot be produced conventionally. Outward effort for peace and justice is fruitful only when it is part of a profound inward change in man's basic awareness of life.

This altered awareness involves new relationships with Truth, with the heavens, with earth, and with other men and women: relationships that would commonly be considered obstacles to the life of achievement, if they were to be considered at all. Indeed, the very word relationship is currently in process of debasement, whereby it is becoming a circumlocution for sexual connection. Most people feel themselves alone so intensely that it is difficult for them to sense the possibility of interacting with anyone else. Any change in established patterns of intellect and emotion appears unimaginable to most Westerners.

And yet it has been widely recognized since early in the twentieth century that these apparently immutable patterns are no more than a matter of cultural choice and not a matter of innate human condition. Indeed, the human condition itself, in various living cultures throughout the world, gives evidence that man's nature is in no way immutably fixed but rather infinitely malleable, and that a wide variety of choices are open alike to people and peoples, particularly since the Western epoch is widely believed to be ending, if it be not ended already.

> Things that flourish fall into decay.
> This is not-Tao,
> And what is not-Tao soon ends.

And the Bible declares the word of the Lord, "Behold I make all things new!"

There is as yet little impetus to see the new things and to follow new paths, even among persons who make much of their lifestyles and pursue, variously, personal meditation, communal living, political activism, sexual latitudinarianism, disordered dress, environmental protection, chemical intoxication, criminal assaults, and terrorist and other agitations. The dead hand of the past is as heavy upon the apparently liberated as it is upon the obviously hidebound. For the essence of conventionality is the belief, so deeply rooted as to be largely unconscious, that the universe revolves around every single human being, that everything that happens must be related first of all to that single being, and that meaning in life is to be found through self-expression and the assertion of self-will. In such will, the bomb-thrower is one with the bible-thumper, the criminal one with the righteous, the reformer one with the unreconstructed. Even the outs are one with the ins, for Western ego-centrism is now being exported with Western technology. There is a new fervor for self-will: in recent decades ego-centrists have been calling for it with the desperations of addicts clamoring for the drugs that kill them.

For such addictions, scriptures of the Way have a simple answer. Lao Tzŭ words it in this manner:

> To know and to be unknowing is best;
> Not to know and to be knowing is sickness.
> Only by being sick of our sickness
> Are we not sick.
> The sage is not sick.
> He is sick of his sickness
> And therefore not sick.

This answer is no different from Isaiah's counsel to turn from serving self to serving God or from Jesus' insistence on saving one's life by losing it and losing one's life by saving it. But the answer cannot be heard clearly until people, everywhere or anywhere, are literally sick of their sickness: sick of trying to establish a personal self over against other selves, sick of seeking to maximize self, sick of clamoring for self-superiority or, what amounts to the same thing, self-inferiority, sick of compulsions, competitions, contests, and the consequent destruction of the true self and of other selves through violent adventurism, psychological or physical or both.

The answer is by no means unfamiliar to Westerners, for prophetic Truth has survived among us, as among most peoples, as a persistent if minor cultural theme, one customarily unnoticed but never entirely forgotten. Truth seems at times to stir in our hearts, informing us without conscious awareness that there are such realities as meaning and affection and the very Truth itself. But it is difficult to act on such promptings if we try to act alone. Even when we become sick of our sickness, we do not get well if we have not the example of other selves to follow. No self gets over self-sickness by its own self.

It is told of Francois de Sales that, when asked how to love God, he counter-questioned, "How does a child learn to walk?" And he explained that a child learns to walk by walking. To anybody but Westerners of do-it-yourself propensities, such a method of self-teaching would appear nonsensical. A child does not learn to walk by himself: he learns to walk by watching the people around him walk. We ourselves can learn to love God only by watching other people love him: or at least by watching their first steps of accepting Truth and becoming mindful of it. Since such activities are nowadays infrequent, alike among those who claim to have found God and those who claim to have found him not, they can be seen most clearly in the scriptures of times past.

> Why did the ancients prize Tao?
> Because if it is sought, it is found.
> Because the guilty are forgiven.

It can be argued that contemporary thought is superior to past thought and that Truth characterizes only the up-to-date. Such are the arguments of Western conventionalism. However dubious their logic, their function is to support the role of self as the center of all that exists. Whether spoken in scientific or religious terms, they have no word concerning the violence that overflows from self-worship — miserable alternative to the worship of the Way — and threatens to engulf the world and consume it. They have no word concerning inward torments of ego that are shaking the mind or with tortures of guilt that are bewildering the emotions. To these things scripture alone speaks.

But here it is essential to distinguish again between those parts of the scriptures which record the voice of the prophets and those parts which are the work of the legalists and the priests, groups who typically seek to institutionalize Truth as well as conventionalize it. Such persons edit the language of the prophets, altering or confusing the original meaning; they add propositions and regulations of their own and make of them a dogmatic literature, misinterpreting or slighting the very word they declare to be unerring, favoring instead contemporary credal constructions, and ignoring in the process the relationship between man and man, the key to man's relationship with God.

Certainly it is natural for anything so important to mankind as the scriptures to be edited, if only to make the original works comprehensible to later generations of men and women. A book that is meaningful enough to be considered inspired is bound to have been rewritten and annotated out of much of its original form: a process that is discernable in our own time in the alterations made in the writings of such men as John Woolman and Mohandas Gandhi. The language of prophetic scripture has to change if its witness to that which does not change is to retain its power. It is not such editing that weakens scripture's impact but rather the revisionism of those publicists who temporize with the changeless by explaining it, in the process adding much of their own, taking away much of the original, and confusing much of the rest.

The imperative task of disentangling scripture from the revision of it is complicated by the necessity of knowing what the whole grain of scripture is before trying to separate the chaff from it. This work is far easier with a scripture foreign to one's own tradition, simply because notions of inerrant sanctity do not attach to it. The work is made still easier with the Tao Teh Ching because many of the later alterations made in its meaning appear in separate volumes of the Taoist canon, there being relatively few in the extant edition of the original book itself.

Explicit in the Tao Teh Ching, moreover, is that sense of reality implicit in all prophetic scripture, a sense that sees the penetration of physical creation by spiritual force: not the existence side-by-side of two distinct realms, but their acting together in the single realm of reality. This interaction is beyond verbal definition to such a degree that it can also be imagined as non-action, the nothing-doing that is one of Lao Tzŭ's major themes. Tao is, indeed, on top of everything as well as into everything, and certainly beyond the names used by scientists, logicians, and other dogmatists to pigeonhole reality. It is everything so much that it is beyond legalisms, beyond rules and observances, beyond morals and legislations, beyond notions of blame and guilt. It is indeed in and beyond everything, just as it is also just *nothing*: the remarkable nothing that penetrates all reality from the space inside atoms and the space that supports and creates stars to that inwardness which is peculiar to mankind and which includes everything human in its nothingness. For it includes spirit and mind, conscious thought and subliminal emotion, in addition to every aspect of the human body in all its own multiplicity. We appear to be, in other words, somethingness in combination with nothingness, in which the somethingness cannot exist without the nothingness, and in which the nothingness often speaks directly to our inward ears in a way that can be described only by analogy:

> Thirty spokes share one hub;
> In emptiness lies the wheel's utility.
> Kneeding clay makes a pot;
> In emptiness lies the pot's utility.
> Cutting doors and windows makes a room,
> In emptiness lies the room's utility.
> Gain can be had from somethingness,
> But use can be had from nothingness.

In the light of such emptiness, Lao Tzŭ records a series of insights into and intimacies with the ways of creation and the ways of man. The insights are in no sense explanations of the universe; they are not ideas or myths or beliefs. They are simply glimpses of what is and records of experiencing what is. Lao Tzǔ's message is not that his readers should believe in what he says in order to achieve a salvation of some sort, but rather that they should accept reality and turn to it, enjoying, as a consequence, inward well-being: a sort of spiritual hedonism in which there is joy and meaning and vitality, however much these may coexist with pain and sorrow and suffering. Tao is the Way in exactly the same manner in which God is Truth.

Like other scriptures of Truth, the book of Tao does not go out of date. It is genuinely open-ended, for its single witness is the reality of Tao, however Tao may manifest itself at one time or another. Set down in writing perhaps in the sixth century B.C., it is a creation of a remarkable time. To that century belong also the writings of Gautama, Jeremiah, and Confucius. But it remains pertinent to all times simply because the Way remains the Way, just as Truth remains Truth, simplicity remains simplicity, non-violence remains non-violence, and the God of these prophetic witnesses remains the God of the prophets.

> If Tao can be Taoed, it's not Tao.
> If its name can be named, it's not its name.
> Has no name: preceeds heaven and earth.
> Has a name: mother of ten thousand things . . . .
> Mystery of mysteries, the door to inwardness!

The way of convention is to give names to all things in the universe out of a petty will to control life. The names may attach to matter or monsters, duties or deities, objects or operations, but they represent an effort to dominate reality through the agency of abstract cogitation. Lao Tzǔ disagrees. "When law and order arose," he writes, "names appeared. Aren't there enough already? Is it not time to stop?" His practice and his counsel is not to name things but to be intimate with them. Truth itself is beyond name, and the name of Tao cannot be its name. Is not God, the God of all the scriptures, forever the One who is nameless and unknown and undefined?

The opposite of naming names is creating paradoxes, and Lao Tzǔ eschews the former and embraces the latter even more fervently than do the writers of other scriptures. Sometimes mistaken for witticism or for a turning upside down of things as they are, paradox provides insight into the awesome inexplicability of life. It is not, of course, to be defined, being hostile to names by nature. It has no laws. It can be described only as it behaves: it repeats apparent opposites again and again so that the veil of words, poor indicators of a reality beyond cogitation, can be rent by the clash of apparently conflicting experience. Paradox cuts across the accumulated thickness of words and illuminates as it flashes. It enlightens where cogitation fails. In ages of bronze or plutonium, it is the only alternative to names.

There can never be a study of it. Look at it, and you will not see it. See it, and you will not have to look at it. Any attempt to describe it, except by paradox, leads nowhere, for it hovers somewhere just at the edge of human understanding. It is like a fleeting motion seen from the corner of the eye only when the eye's center is focused elsewhere. Only one definitive statement can be made about it, and that is that it is not really paradoxical. For Lao Tzŭ celebrated rather than analyzed the mysteriousness of life. He did not wonder about the universe but felt wonder towards it. He responded with awe, conveyed without logic simply through a series of affirmations of what is omnipresent both in the heavens and in the hearts of men and women and children.

Paradox is perplexing to Westerners brought up on names. To such persons Lao Tzŭ can seem lacking in pertinence because lacking in familiarity. The commentary that accompanies this translation is designed to familiarize the Western reader with Tao and to further his acquaintance by suggesting Tao's pertinence to him in his own time and place. But once the commentary has provided such introduction, it can be put aside. Lao Tzŭ's meaning is best assimilated by repetitive reading. Prophecy and paradox speak best for themselves.

> True words are not nice;
> Nice words are not true.
> A good man does not argue;
> An arguer is not good.
> The wise are not learned;
> The learned are not wise.

The intent of the Tao Teh Ching is to speak about the unspeakable, and, as Lao Tzŭ points out, "He who speaks does not know, and he who knows does not speak." In reading about Tao, it is wise to sense the possibility and even the necessity of being intimate with the Reality which it would be presumptuous to understand. Lao Tzŭ is close to Tao with an intimacy he recommends across the ages to us.

2. The Failure of Success

It is the experience of Lao Tzŭ that it is natural for men, women, and children to turn to Tao, and that it is separation from Tao which is unnatural. Turning-toward is life; turning-away is death; and the choice is so momentous that the experience of it exceeds all conventional understanding of good and evil, just as Tao itself is so awesome that it goes beyond all customary descriptions of divinity and all customary methods of organizing society. Once there is turning-toward, there is holding-onto; and holding onto Tao is radically different from believing in myths that explain the universe and enforce conventional moralities of sin and guilt. Tao is not a subject of belief and observance but of direct and factual experience, both of inward and outward reality, which Tao fuses in much the same manner as it brings together the poles of paradox into a unitary flash of insight. Like the Kingdom of Heaven, the Way is outside us but found within us.

> Heaven abides; earth lasts.
> They last and abide
> By not living for themselves.
> Hence they live forever.

The Way being within us, we have only to follow inward direction to follow Tao as heaven and earth follow. Tao has nothing to do with that celestial manipulation of man and nature wherein higher powers intervene in the normal courses of life to make special events happen or not happen. Tao, to be sure, is indeed the ultimate Reality toward whose completeness man, earth, and heaven move. But it is first of all the path along which they travel. Being on the path is as life-giving as reaching the end of it, while being off the path is more death-dealing than ignorance of where the path leads.

> If I have a grain of wisdom,
> I walk along the great Tao
> And only fear to stray.

For the Tao Teh Ching is as negative concerning man and the universe as it is positive and as positive as it is negative. The horror of straying is as tremendous as the wonder of finding, and Lao Tzŭ, in common with

other prophetic writers, seldom mentions the one condition without imply-
ing at least the other. Indeed, the one seems to come from the other,
since moving toward Tao is typically one consequence of being away. It
is important to understanding the Tao Teh Ching to avoid explaining any
part of it conceptually, since all parts of it emphasize an experience
of life that is inherently non-conceptual. Let it be said here simply
that people are driven to the comfort of health by the pain of sickness.

The first impact, therefore, of the Tao Teh Ching — even in its
positive passages — is negative. How sick sick people are!

> On tiptoe you don't stand.
> Astride you don't walk.
> Showing yourself, you don't shine.
> Asserting yourself, you don't show.
> Boasting yourself won't get you credit.
> Vaunting yourself won't let you endure.
> In Tao, these things are called
> Tumors and dregs, which all things abhor.
> Whoever has Tao does not dwell on them.

When the Tao Teh Ching is used as a critique of our contemporary
time of troubles, it is evident that the troubles result not from a series
of particular ills but from an attitude toward reality wherein people
desert Tao and try to find meaning and motivation in their own selves, or,
by self-projection, within their own groups, which can enhance the value
of self by devaluing outsiders. Indeed, man's false view of himself, in
which he sees himself as the center of the universe, is the key not only
to Lao Tzŭ's denunciation of success but also to his praise of Tao. If
a man does not follow Tao, or in Western terms worship God, he will have
nothing to follow and nothing to worship but himself. The deceit of this
idolatry is so pernicious that it becomes a sickness. Other sicknesses of
opulence and oppression and violence, whether expressed in hatred of
others and a will to stand supreme, or in self-hatred and a will to be overwhelmed, spring from this central deceit.

The positive response to the deceit, in Western terms, is to love
and do as you please. Lao Tzŭ says:

> Twist and get whole.
> Bend and get straight.
> Be empty and get filled.
> Be worn and get renewed.
> Have little: get much.
> Have much: get confused.

> The sage . . . does not show himself,
> Hence he shines.

Does not assert himself,
Hence he is seen.
Does not boast his merits,
Hence he gets credit.
Does not vaunt himself,
Hence he survives.
Does not compete with anyone,
Hence no one beneath heaven
Can compete with him.

The old saying,
The twisted shall be made whole,
Is it not true?
Be whole and you will return.

This counsel of wholeness can indeed be followed in times of noise and alarms, but it is no prescription for self-discovery or self-fulfillment. Nor is Lao Tzǔ a mystic in the sense of taking man out of this world to cling to a supermundane deity. Rather Lao Tzǔ sees the link between the reality men and women live by and turn to in their daily lives to be inseparable from the way by which their lives in the outside world are organized. Change the world, you do not thereby change man, and you therefore make no more than superficial changes in the world. Change man, who is infinitely malleable, you change the world.

But there can be no change, individual or social, until men and women are sick enough of self-will to recognize what they are sick with. Otherwise self-will is dismissed as something other people are sick with. Yet even in matters of apparent triviality like the weather, it is everywhere epidemic. The rain, for instance, rains first of all on me. It is so personal to me that I am in a perverse relationship with it, so that it will fall if I don't carry an umbrella, hold off if I do: a line of reasoning I recognize to be slightly ridiculous, but one which I am willing to own to even publicly, with suitably wry humor, out of simple but satisfying self-gratification.

At places of work, shop and office politics are commonly held to be the acts of people of unusually self-centered will. And yet we recognize, through our acquaintance with triumph and failure, that these are places for us, not less than others, to measure our selves against other selves. We seek the status of telling other people what to do; we try to avoid the non-status of being told. When possible, we denigrate the labor of others, if only in our own minds, in favor of our own. We show off. We gossip. We constantly compare. We conspire to have ourselves recognized and others overlooked. Unless, of course, we are aware of the enticements of low-ego, whereby self-will feeds on self-denigration.

Indeed, it makes little difference whether we assert ourselves or deprecate ourselves, so long as attention is focused on ourselves, whether we are sublimely confident or miserably depressed. Nothing focuses attention more forcefully on self than a state of guilt, misery, and general inadequacy. Establishing supremacy often fails, but establishing inferiority always succeeds. Deceits of this sort lead men and women to interpose compulsions and evasions and escapes, not to mention fantasies and compulsions and combats, between themselves and reality: to such a degree, indeed, that it is difficult to distinguish fact from self-will, a state of affairs hardly conducive to work or play.

This situation reverses Lao Tzŭ's saying,

> [The sage] does not compete with anyone,
> And no one beneath heaven can compete with him.

Restated for today, this couplet would read,

> Because you compete with others,
> Everyone will certainly compete with you.

The consequence is not only competition but also hostility compounded with fear. Places of work have more and more become testing grounds for measuring self against self, arenas for winning sympathy or nursing inferiority, and theatres of hidden conflict and innuendo, in which it is necessary to guard constantly against threats, reprimands, cabals, warnings, and slurs. The enormity of the hidden hostility that pervades offices, schools, and factories is widely overlooked because most people choose not to see beyond the injustices with which they are personally visited. Beyond personal hurt lies a system of semi-organized hostility, in which there is open approval of aggressive self-serving without any economic or pedagogical or organizational purposes. Large enterprise actually functions on the basis of cooperation not competition. Yet work becomes an occasion to pit self-will against self-will.

Such encounter is generally known to be confusing, painful, and exhausting. Yet people still insist on being treated well, while they dream of treating other people ill, an insistence that simply intensifies the encounter. Sometimes hostility rises no higher in intensity than is required to judge others and gossip about them, but not infrequently it erupts in anger and informs us that hostility is indeed an overwhelming urge, not simply a device to achieve superiority or to reinforce inferiority or to do both at once, but also a device to give expression to self, even if the self be alone, withdrawn, and miserable.

> Nothing beneath heaven
> Is softer and weaker than water.
> Nothing is better
> To attack the hard and strong
> And nothing can take its place.

> The weak overcome the strong;
> The soft overcome the hard.
> There is no one beneath heaven
> Who doesn't know this,
> And no one who practices it . . . .
> Indeed straight words seem crooked!

If, again negatively, we look at ourselves at home, we confront an hostility that forces us to defame the people with whom we live rather than admit our own self-sickness: nothing is wrong with us; something is wrong with, say, the family. Men and women seek closeness, find aloofness; they wish to give love and receive it, but often settle for no more than the projected centeredness on self shown in the narcissistic condition of being in love. Too close to receive and too shackled to give affection, they attempt to be recipients of their own love: a hopeless try since it is futile to receive without giving and impossible to give to self without having given to others.

Without mutuality, a household can come to resemble not so much the barnyard — cattle, sheep, and pigs at least huddle and wallow together — as the chicken coop, in which place individuals busy themselves pecking and being pecked. Who shall be top chicken? Who shall cluck at whom? Who shall strut in front of what? Such questions are settled not by an inward look at self-sickness but by its projection into group life, and the answer is proclaimed that something outside self is wrong, perhaps that ancient device of mutual help, the family. The will to undercut one's spouse, to enlarge gaps between generations, to dominate one's childen, to get even with one's parents, deceiving the old and training the young in new deceits (when not actually abusing them), using humor to cut at others, playing roles of consequence in the lives of people nearby, and finding common ground occasionally in gossiping about and contending with other human groupings: all this hen-like hostility is tolerated without realizing that it is literally inhuman. Indeed, all the pettiness and tawdriness and miserable ineptitude of self-will is so contrary to humanity that any human being can give it up whenever he is willing to do so. "Abandon righteousness," advises Lao Tzŭ, "and the people will go back to natural affection." Righteous self-love is not natural; ordinary humble goodness is.

While interchange between family members survives, at least as a means of vocalizing hostilities, conversation as the ancient mainstay of household pleasure has given way to solitary pursuits, in particular the watching of television, which appears to be a cultural choice of a people who have determined that dialogue must at all costs be killed. It is only incidentally the function of television to tell lies, stimulate fears, enthrall with violence, and besot the emotions. The prime function of television is simply to keep people watching television. It is a projected self that makes it difficult to do at home anything other than keeping to one's self and savoring the artificial spice of canned hostility.

Hostility nowadays is said to have invaded the bed chamber, where affection was long believed to prevail. Some three hundred years ago, in a pamphlet pleading against government cruelty and religious intolerance, William Penn wrote, "Nothing but kindness keeps up the human race. Men and women don't get children in spite of but because of affection. 'Tis wonderful to think by what friendly and gentle ways nature produces and matures the creatures of this world." We are now informed by not a few students of the emotions that hostility is more important in the sexual act than affection. And we are assured by not a few students of eroticism that solitary sex is more gratifying than partner sex, and that partner sex itself needs enhancing by sex of a group or semi-group sort, whether practiced all at once or in series.

How much sexual latitudinarianism has increased in incidence is unknown, but the publicity given to it has increased greatly. It would seem that there is a growing interest in sex with unknown persons who excite because of their unfamiliarity (let alone in solitary sex and hostile sex) and a preference for it over sex with known persons for whom affection can be felt. This preference can hardly be possible except among persons who want to interact with themselves. Sexual relationships with a multitude of people or with a succession of people appear to be little more than relationships with a variety of organs and thus little more than symptoms of the anti-eroticism that has so long characterized Western civilization, according to whose conventions people are supposed to be splendidly single and not close to one another.

Happily, people are not what they are supposed to be. But neither are they what they are capable of being. While most men and women have unconscious acquaintance with the Way sufficient to make them shun the more drastic departures from it, they generally remain blind to the deep lodgment of hostility and willfullness and fear within them. Men and women have really only two alternatives: to follow the Way or not to follow it. To follow it somewhat more than persons who actively shun it, as do men of outward selfishness and violence, may harm fewer people but does little to increase inward well-being or decrease social evil. Ordinary ego-centrics are not less miserable than extreme ones, and their misery is no less contagious. For inward misery, be it remembered, is the chief consequence of straying from Tao, not simply blame and guilt.

Of those who actively shun Tao, Lao Tzŭ says:

> The great Tao is easy indeed,
> But the people choose by-paths.
> The court is very resplendent;
> Very weedy are the fields,
> And the granaries very empty.
> They wear gaudy clothes,
> Carry sharp swords,

> Exceed in eating and drinking,
> Have riches more than they can use.
> Call them robber-braggarts;
> They are anti-Tao indeed!

This denunciation hits at the people in any epoch, not alone the early Chinese epoch, who are autocratic, competitive, self-conscious, class-conscious, superstitious, deceitful, violent, and oppressive. But the denunciation extends also to those persons who are opposed precisely to these characteristics. Interposing good causes between oneself and Tao is not much different in its inward effects from interposing bad causes. In our days of compulsively neurotic interposition, those who chase after good causes are much more numerous than those who chase after bad ones. Indeed, one measure of the inward crisis that grips so many people is the failure of good-intending, self-intending individuals to find themselves in any causes, whatever their nature.

Indeed, the search for self — the self that is ecstatic or the self that is miserable — distracts attention from the true path along which such good things as justice and peace are to be found, and it breeds, when they are not found, fear, rage, guilt, depression, aloneness, alienation, and deceit. Even when the self becomes dubious about success on individual terms and seeks it in dedication to gurus and groups, it still follows its failed fantasies and resentments and compulsions and competitions. The mind is set to work to keep reality away and, mindless of its devices, is left at the mercy of unconscious posturings.

> When Tao is lost, there is virtue.
> When virtue is lost, there is humaneness.
> When humaneness is lost, there is morality.
> When morality is lost, there is ceremony.
> Now ceremony is the shell
> Of loyalty and trust
> And the beginning of confusion.

For what is less than Tao is not more than confusion.

In the pursuit of good ends, success fails not alone because means and ends are out of harmony but because the inward drive that underlies both means and ends is out of harmony with life, with Tao. The very notion of success, in the sense of gathering power for a good purpose and using it to achieve that purpose, means more often than not the failure of the good purpose. When success is used consciously as a means, it is usually sought unconsciously as an end: some such end as taking intellectual stances or moral positions that serve as secret advertisements for one's self. The power that is sought to make these positions prevail is not so much the power to get things done as it is the power to tell other people what to do, not so much for making other people free as for making them do what is good for them, not so much for casting down unrighteousness as for displaying self-righteousness. When other persons try to foist their intellectual, social, or moral convictions upon us, we see their hidden motivations clearly, but when we do the same, we fail to recognize even the foisting.

The fascination with power among people of libertarian intention lies in the fact that power is the act of impressing one's own will or the will of one's group on others, regardless of the size of the issues involved, be they large ones of state or small ones of daily life. An obvious power play is manipulating children to act affectionately instead of demonstrating how to go about being affectionate. When affection fails at home, just as when peace fails abroad, the answer is more power. Few peace-making parents are alert to their tyranny over their offspring.

Let me take as example a personal conviction about peace. I am stricken by the possibility of atomic destruction and convinced that it is increased by armaments and threats of war. To help break the chain of violence that links humankind to war, I insist that my mental analysis of violence bred by violence be accepted by enough people to force those in power to change their minds. And I argue for my understanding of past history, current events, and future projections. I undertake to gather large crowds of marching and shouting demonstrators, and I court publicity for them, hopefully television publicity. I parade with colorful signs and striking costumes. I orate emotionally; I call names; I demonstrate; I stir fear. I tell other people what to do. But other people, precisely the other people whose minds I seek to alter, see very clearly that what I am really seeking is the power to become a celebrity, an authority figure, and a self-righteous prig who knows what is good for other people and is simply going to put other people down. Lao Tzŭ writes:

> Give up wisdom, abandon knowledge,
> And the people will benefit a hundredfold.
> Give up benevolence, abandon righteousness,
> And the people will go back to natural affection.
> Give up cunning, abandon gain,
> And robbers and thieves will disappear.

In self-righteousness lies the final failure of success. The call of all the prophetic teachers is for goodness, but when goodness is measured against the goodness of other people, it ceases to be good and becomes divisive and self-righteous. Faced with such alternatives, the true prophets choose not to succeed. They fail not alone in worldly terms, but even in terms of their goal of turning people to Truth. They fail repeatedly. Their true victories, which belong not to them but to Truth itself, arise out of their repeated failures. Moses emerges as an awesome teacher, for example, not in spite of but because of the series of repeated setbacks he suffers tragically in the midst of the desert wanderings as he tries to lead the people to a new sense of God; and at the very end of the wandering he fails even to gain entry into the promised land. Jeremiah cries out, "Seekest thou great things; seek them not," and finds himself outcast by men who "oppress and oppress, deceive and deceive." Gautama was so much a failure that he turned his back on his own courts and palaces. And Jesus, who aimed his teaching at the poor and unlettered, spoke harshly of the self-righteous and was so little a success that he suffered the death of a criminal.

Himself a dropout and probably a castoff, Lao Tzŭ too rejected success and found, in common with other teachers like him, victory in the simple reality of the Way, that Way by which man can be healed inwardly in his dealings with others and outwardly through the realization of it in the outward world. Once the way is sensed, things inward and outward fit readily into place. Men and women look within themselves and look outside themselves, and in both directions they see purpose and direction and meaning in life.

Perhaps this is a victory that can come to every person who learns to know the failure of success. When Tao is shunned, men and women look within themselves and find nothing more than a meaninglessness they try to overcome through self-awareness, consciousness-raising, and other egocentric stirrings that prompt them to seek success. Primarily, that search is a search for meaning, for something that will justify them in their lives and confirm them in their beings. But when the search leads to a power over others that can be supported only by the illusion of self-righteousness, the attractiveness of success is seen as illusion; success itself finally fails; and search must be started elsewhere. For righteousness is more and more widely seen as a cloak worn on top of success and failure, praise and blame by people who are trying to hide the tawdriness of their undergarments. Out of these torments, there can come a new attitude toward life and a new way of life.

> The great Tao flows everywhere;
> It can go to the right or the left.
> The ten thousand things draw life from it,
> And it does not deny them.
> It completes its work, but takes no title.
> It clothes and feeds the ten thousand things.
> But does not own them.
> You can call it small.
> The ten thousand things return to it,
> But it does not own them.
> You can call it great.
>
> Because it does not seek to be great,
> Its greatness is accomplished.

3. Nothing-Doing

The alternative to success is *nothing-doing,* not a negative restraint and a holding back from life, but a moving forward and a reaching out to the beyond-words reality of Tao. Nothing-doing is actually a way of getting things done; it is also the only way of doing them with the vigor and persuasiveness that results from following the Way. It is not an upside down bit of humor. Lao Tzǔ says flatly:

> Do nothing-doing
> And everything will get done.

In Chinese, the very character for action reflects distaste for fussy interference with life. Commentators point out that its ancient form appears to have been derived from a representation of a man trying to pull an elephant around by the nose.

But nothing-doing means more than avoiding interference. Negatively, it means not projecting self as the center of all that happens, not impressing one's will on events, not manipulating people and things, not devising grandiose plans or sequences of plans, or simply not combatting other people, not violating nature, not destroying things, not murdering people. *Something-doing,* which to Lao Tzǔ is virtually synonymous with violence, comes from self-will, which is false to the Way, false to nature, false to the nature of man.

Positively, nothing-doing means something so vital and profound that it is not to be talked about. It is inherent in the spiritual-physical reality of Tao that pervades all things and all beings, that makes events fruitful by not channeling them but by freeing them: the reality that creates history not out of the decisions of a controlling few but out of the thoughts and actions of everyone alive. Nothing-doing even provides a compelling means of communicating, whereby what a man is and does speaks louder than what he says. In the long run, nothing-doing always wins over something-doing, but its workings are best described by analogy with soft things like water which wear away all hardness.

> The softest things beneath heaven
> Overcome the hardest.
> Nothingness alone penetrates no space.
> Hence I know the use of nothing-doing.

In the something-doing West, that which is natural is held suspect, for there it is believed that it is natural for nature to be violent and natural for man to lie, steal, and kill. Hence man is to be prevented from following his "natural" urges by systems of praise and blame, reward and punishment, manipulation and restraint. Personal violence can be prevented, it is believed, only by organized violence, and it is believed further that this organized violence alone has civilized man and brought him out of a slavery in which he is thought by inclination to have assaulted, raped, and robbed whomever he met. This comic-strip view of man as a club-wielding animal would be amusing did it not coincide with popular (and, for a long time, philosophical) views of savagery as something that modern man has had to rise above through the agencies of churches, courts, and prisons.

Such a view is witness to the pathetic attempt of Western ego-centrics to cloak themselves in the garments of righteousness. Stone-age people, who were still the common people of the bronze-age times in which Lao Tzǔ wrote, were an essentially simple (and essentially matrilocal) people, incapable of projecting self as the center of all that happens, and recent research into prehistory suggests them to be remarkably free of wars and oppressions. They seem to have been dependent on and delighted by daily sustenance, ordinary quiet, familial conversation, and common affection, as are not a few country peoples, hill peoples, rain-forest peoples, and island peoples still alive today. To be sure, they were undoubtedly very dirty, diseased, short-lived, and extremely superstitious. Undoubtedly they gave way at times to theft, violence, and other forms of selfishness. But they did not organize theft and violence into a manner of living, and they knew nothing about the neurotic involvements of self-will. Indeed, it is from these simpler patterns of living that men and women may have come to recognize the Way, while it is from the far-different patterns of the ages of bronze and iron that they may have developed notions of self-willed violence and deceit.

Of the prophetic voices raised against organized violence, Lao Tzǔ's is one of the earliest:

> He who uses Tao to guide rulers of men
> Does not force beneath-heaven with arms.
> Such things recoil on their users.
>
> Where armies are
> Briars and brambles grow.
> Bad harvests follow big wars.
> Be firm and that is all:
> Dare not rely on force.
> Be firm and not haughty,
> Firm but not boastful,
> Firm but not proud,

Firm when necessary,
Firm but non-violent.

What others have taught, I also teach:
Men of violence come to death by violence.
Whoever said this is my teacher.

Today's new man of violence is one who sees death as the consequence of the outward violence that other men perpetuate, and not as the consequence of the inward violence that he practices unawares himself. He is fascinated with international adventurism of the Bay of Pigs sort. He amuses himself with wildly romantic international spy stories of improbable but egocentric bent. He is often avid for details about the possible scope of atomic destruction. And he is stirred by the contemporary equivalent of saber-rattling which involves nonsensical talk about the tactical use of instruments of annhilation and about survival through the employment of them. Something-doing can produce a marked headiness of emotion. The new man of violence can experience the bravura of threats and declamations and can thrill to the luxuriant adrenalism of fear and anger, and at the same time be strongly opposed to war in his own mind: as is practically everyone today, including the professional military.

Only he never observes to himself what is obvious to himself — and to practically everyone of every shade of political opinion — that the nation-state as Westerners have known it for about half a millenium is suddenly at an end. It cannot make its will prevail internationally — not to protect its citizens or advance its interests or secure its sources of raw materials — without in effect committing suicide. The nation-state of yesterday is possible today only for a few emerging third-world countries who fight or threaten to fight only amongst themselves, and even this limited form of statism is seen as a threat to world peace. But the nation-state is not openly recognized as a dead end, and the urgency of finding other instruments to take its place is seldom felt and never acted on. Centuries of something-doing have resulted in nothing done.

An important use of the Tao Teh Ching is to help Westerners recognize the hidden attraction to violence that makes them blind to the most ordinary and most obvious dangers of it, ranging from self-destruction to universal annihilation. Clearly this attraction is part of the self-worship of me-first egocentrism. It is also part of the fear and violence that results from the combative atmosphere of daily living and, notably, of daily playing. Even our amusements are steeped in anxiety and shot through with conflict, as shown in sports, advertisements, soap operas, television dramas, horror movies, war-to-be movies, suspense stories supposed to be comic, murder stories supposed to be more entertaining than the old love stories, and the new nonfiction that celebrates violence commingled with sex and hate, not to mention the animal shows on television with their heavy emphasis on the fearfulness of animals eating animals. It is

impossible to have one's emotions played up and down upon by such enter-
tainment without losing all sense that violence is a danger and all feeling
that there is such a thing as spiritual reality.

The fear and violence of crime are not dissimilar from the fear and
violence of war. They attract, they fascinate, they preoccupy: not
simply those persons who are actively involved but also those who are
passive onlookers. Lao Tzŭ suggests that these two groups are linked,
psychologically rather than causally:

> When people are hard to govern,
> Their rulers are something-doing.
> That is why they are hard to govern.

That is to say, the poor commit crime beeause the rich not only expect
them to but also, perversely, want them to: a perversity still common today.
Wanted, more or less consciously, by dominant groups is a social system
that rewards rapacity while providing obstacles to being raped, and that
at the same time permits enough rape to keep people. generally athrill
with fear, violence, and self-righteousness. This latter condition is
possible only when the righteous have the unrighteous to click their
tongues over. What is better to click over than criminality? The crime
of punishment, says psychiatrist Karl Menninger in his book by that title,
is precisely this self-righteousness admixed with hidden guilt for secret
unrighteousness. Small wonder that crime provides the principal content
of the various media. In contemporary social systems, bottom-drawer people
serve to justify top-drawer people in their position, and criminals are
everywhere considered the lowest people in the bottom drawer. Besides,
they are also misapprehended as including other groups of outcasts, who
being thought criminal, can be treated as non-people.

There are other dramas of immorality that incite to crime. A principal
one is the universal demonstration of the something-doing success-involved
self. The actuality of violence in the home and on the streets arises
from that egocentrism not less than does the possibility of violence
abroad. Crime nowadays reflects less the material plight of the necessi-
tous (badly supplied with goods but probably less badly than at previous
times in history), and more the will of the underdog to have his self
gratified, or at least exercised, as effectively as the overdog's. As a
criminal motive, self-expression has now more push than cupidity.

Defacing nature, destroying property, thieving goods, and setting
fire to cities (the very cities to which people flocked for more than
seven centuries to find a new life and a new culture): all these are
essentially acts of self-assertion and of establishing oneself as a something instead of a nothing. Mugging and murder, in which victor directly
confronts victim, are dramatic acts of establishing superiority. Even if
the victor is caught, he may still get on television, and this event is
almost universally considered the pinnacle of contemporary recognition of

self. Murder has become what philosopher Thomas Hobbes thought it to be, the ultimate equalizer. Nothing more grotesquely illustrates the intoxication of success, the inward swagger of it, the upthrust of physical sensation, the flooding of adrenaline, the bloodrush of conquest.

Emotions experienced by the criminal can be experienced vicariously by those who only fear they will be his victims. Compelling indeed are the visceral sensations stirred by fascination for violence. It may well be that the current high levels of criminality represent the cultural choice of a people who do not want to be deprived of the something-doing of daily violence, even though the prisons overflow and the rate of crime goes up until society progressively becomes unable to protect itself. Efforts to decrease crime seem actually to multiply it. Democratic countries have made such great and futile efforts, both in increasing the quantities of laws and in enlarging the size of the legal and penal system that their criminal controls far exceed those of any of the oriental despotisms of times past. Lao Tzŭ, by contrast, says:

> The more laws and orders there are,
> The more thieves and robbers appear. . . .
> Do nothing and the people of themselves reform.

For Westerners, it is more attractive to do something. A marked reduction in current crime could be effected almost overnight by state sale rather than gangster sale of drugs to addicts, but this alternative is held to be an unrighteous coddling of outcasts, while the idea that crime could be discouraged by decreased popular usage of legal drugs like alcohol (a factor in probably a majority of all crimes) would be held impertinent. It would seem that people who are not criminals insist on living in such a way that there is no way not to have criminals.

> Don't exalt the worthy:
> People then will not compete.
> Don't prize rare goods:
> People then will not steal.
> Don't show what is covetable:
> The people's hearts won't be upset. . . .
> [The sage] leads the people
> To not-know and not-want
> And the cunning ones to dare not do.
> By doing-nothing, everything is set in order.

This prophetic Way — for it is also the way of such teachers as Isaiah, Gautama, and Jesus — is specifically denounced by self-appointed terrorists and supposed revolutionaries who believe that eggs should be broken Lenin-like to make their particular omelets. Conspiracies of misguided violence have long held romantic attractions to Westerners who want to grasp the world and mold it to their own image, at the personal sacrifice of love, life, liberty, and even common honesty. Attempts of this sort at social change are so weighted down with the conventionalisms of self and violence that very little change can take place. Usually nothing can take place at all except wretched criminality. Filled with awe for themselves, the terrorists, the ultranationalists, the separatists, and the other dividers of people exalt their emotion with a frenzied violence that can be described only as utter reaction. Striking sparks in a dynamite factory is hardly progressive. Indeed, nothing can any longer be considered as reactionary as violence, together with the something-doing that is the basis for it. For the problem goes beyond terrorism to the something-doing of people who want to impress their will on the world. It is the something-doing that infects not only the terrorist but the street punk and not only the punk but the citizen who dreams of gore.

But there is another way:

> Tao never does anything
> And everything gets done.
> If rulers can keep to it,
> All things will change of themselves.

> Nature speaks little.
> Squalls do not last the morning,
> Nor downpours the day.
> What stirs them up?
> Heaven and earth!
> Even heaven and earth
> Does not long make a fuss.
> How much less should men?

The Way works in all aspects of life, personal and social. How it works is a futile question, for the Way is something to walk on and not to think about. For nothing-knowing, says Lao Tzŭ, is a key part of nothing-doing. And that is another chapter.

4. Nothing-Knowing

Just as the fussiness of something-doing leads Lao Tzŭ to uphold nothing-doing, so does the fuzziness of something-knowing lead him to applaud nothing-knowing: an emptiness of mind akin to the selflessness of speech in the famous quotation, "He who speaks does not know; he who knows does not speak." Nothing-knowing has to do with more than self. A key to the ultimate nothingness, it has to do with creation, how it is and how it may be experienced.

> Do nothing-doing.
> Manage nothing-managing; taste nothing-tasting.
> Exalt the low; multiply the few.
> Requite hatred with virtue.

Elsewhere, Lao Tzŭ's counsel is more personal: "Give up learning and you will have no anxieties." And he contrasts the hopeful condition of "stupid stupid" with the hopeless condition of "clever clever."

To most Western scholars, such language suggests distaste for the edifices of intellect they inhabit, and it is conventional for those of them who know anything about the Tao Teh Ching to dismiss it as mystical and quietist and mindlessly subjective. And yet it is not mystical in the sense of seeking absorption in the All; nor is it quietist in the sense of withdrawing from the here and now. Written in the form of a handbook on how to govern (possibly because those who governed were then the only people who knew how to read), it is intensely social in its purposes and dedicated to the well-being of commoners, not the power of rulers. The book, morever, is obdurately factual. Lao Tzŭ treats *what is* as inviolate, avoids subjectivity, and turns his back ahead of time on the superstition that later Taoism embraced. Subjectivity and superstition result from relating reality to one's self and trying to control it, while factuality results from relating to Tao and avoiding any effort at control.

The Tao of Lao Tzŭ is reality without seams, with no separations of any sort between natural fact and spiritual fact, both so commingled in the whole of Tao as to have no separate significance. It is whole. It is not a patchwork quilt of diverse theories that try to explain the universe and make it intelligible to beings of limited intellects.

But to reason thus is to turn an introduction of Lao Tzŭ into a cogitation about him. The book of Tao, like Tao itself, is to be known by nothing-knowing, by being open to it, by absorbing it, by becoming intimate with it, not by building mental constructions on top of it.

> Without going out of the door
> You can know beneath-heaven.
> Without looking out of the window
> You can see heaven's way.
> The farther you go,
> The less you know.
>
> Thus the Sage
> Knows without walking,
> Sees without looking,
> And does without doing.

This is the wholeness of Tao.

But unless there be that wholeness, unless there be Tao or Truth or whatever other designation shall be given to undivided reality, then absoluteness of fact is only too easily compromised by the ego-centrism of the observer. Indeed, the Tao Teh Ching penetrates sharply into the confusions of our Faustian way of thinking. However remarkable may be the results of the scientific method in the realm of practicality, in the realm of actuality the method can be vitiated by a will to control nature through understanding it, conceptualizing it, cogitating it, cutting it down to human size, and subjecting it to the operations of one aspect of man's being, his intellect. Knowledge is thus given an ego spin, and remarkable simplifications and personalizations often result.

Such departures from factuality have been chronicled for more than sixty years by students of the history of ideas. The consequences include arguing ahead of the facts, elaborating on the basis of limited facts, treating mathematics not as a tool but as itself a fact, assuming that facts too distant to be examined are structured the same as facts close at hand, and — particularly important today — imposing unconscious personal imaginings upon factual reality.

Projection of this sort may be nothing more than an attempt of a conventional sort to explain nature. But it may also be gross deceit in the form of misstatement of fact, and it may be made, as even the daily newspapers have reported, to further personal interests in scientific investigation. Reported have been frauds involving biological and psychological research; the frauds seem to be spreading. In some cases, the intention to deceive is hidden, statistical manipulation being used, sometimes unconsciously, to make data prove what the investigator started out to prove. But in other cases, the raw data themselves are falsified. Deceit of this sort can be self-deceit. If I hold that facts are not sacred, I can find myself at the mercy of the notion that the universe is not meaningful but that I am, and that I can make of everything precisely what I will. It is difficult, indeed, to be in a relationship with even simple everyday facts without being in a relationship to an ultimate Truth from which a fact emerges to be exactly as it is. The egocentric choice, of course, is to gather more and more data and have it pertain less and less to anything beyond self. Hence:

> To get learning, add to it daily.
> To get Tao, subtract daily.

In some areas where data are quantified, notably the sciences that are called social, fad and opinion hold sway, and investigators are known for the positions they take rather than for the facts they discover. And when social science turns into social action, ideological purity, whereby a man stands unshakable wherever he stands, is valued above facts. Such purity resembles orthodoxy so closely that it may well be theology's offspring. The purists inform me that God will be wroth if I, one small unit in the large human race, do not declare acceptance with mind and will of a series of their abstractions about him.

Such misuse of fact leads to calling things by name: scientific things like atoms, natural things like genera, divine things like theologies, and human things like behavior patterns. A considerable part of human learning amounts to little more than a pigeonholing of reality, very much in the manner of the stone-age people who sought to control things by knowing their secret names and by intoning the names under proper conditions and in a suitable sequence. Trying to control reality by naming it — or by having a special vocabulary for describing it — is so unappealing to Lao Tzŭ and using names to exalt self is so abhorrent that his teaching may indeed be said to consist simply of not having names.

> Tao is always without name,
> Simple and small . . . .
>
> When law and order arose,
> Names appeared.
> Aren't there enough already?
> Is it not time to stop?

When naming things nowadays, it is frequently possible to reinforce the names with numbers and thus to further the illusion of control over things. Or over people. Through intelligence tests, aptitude tests, and psychological tests, the names of the characteristics of each individual can be derived from the numerical position he occupies on a master code of rank. This position can then be used to determine the future of every human being as regards educational success, personal adjustment, and business and professional advancement. Thus are the superstitions of name and number ritualistically linked. But the consequence of such illusion is violence to fact and violence to the human beings subjected to it.

Consider, for instance, the new numerical nomenclature of the American Psychiatric Association, which recently brought out a third version of its formidably titled "Diagnostic and Statistic Manual of Mental Disorders," the so-called DSM-III, a code that is supposed to rationalize the care of the mentally ill. Essentially it is a ritualistic device that will complicate present treatment of psychiatric problems and confuse research into future treatments, but will do so in such a tidy numerical way as to suggest progress in mental health. The rationale of the code is to provide hundreds of numbered names and computerized numbers that are supposed to coincide with actual disease entities, and that can be used, first, as a basis for deciding treatment, second, as a method of research, and — when combined with a numerical scale of severity — third, hospitalization and accreditation, and, fourth, insurance reimbursement.

But nobody knows whether there are any such things as specific disease entities in psychiatry; many experienced practitioners hold that there is rather a spectrum of symptoms with one set of symptoms fusing into the next without fixed boundaries. Patients are not this, that, or the other; they behave in this way, that way, or the other way. Factual symptoms rather than conceptual diagnoses provide, therefore, the best basis for treatment and research. In a conceptualized system, the patient gets lost and insight gets suppressed. There is not a need to categorize, not a need to judge, compare, contrast, and subject to theory. Rather there is a need to be present and to be open to whatever is going on. Individual man, whether he is out of his mind or in it, is not much more understandable than the Tao from which he springs.

When Lao Tzŭ says that "not to know and to be knowing is sickness", is he not referring to that which is indeed beyond cogitation and beyond every attempt at knowledgeability? He is no enemy of all knowing. Indeed, he emphasizes that "to know and to be unknowing is best." Rather he is the enemy of exactly that sort of knowledgeability which denaturalizes and dehumanizes life and make of itself deceit. *Clever* is his word for it, and the word he sets in opposition to it is *stupid*. The stupid man clings to Tao; the clever man turns away.

> Why are the people hard to govern?
> Because they are too clever.
> Clever government is a curse.
> Not-clever government a blessing.
> To know these two things
> Is to follow the ancient pattern,
> And to know the ancient pattern
> Is original virtue.
> Original virtue is far-reaching and deep.
> It leads all things
> Back to the great harmony.

Nowhere has the Tao Teh Ching better demonstrated its social utility than in its critique of cleverness. It is the habit of governments to outfox themselves, and over the dynasties the simple teachings of Lao Tzǔ have helped Chinese governments pause long enough to rescue themselves from at least some of the consequences of overreaching themselves. Western governments overreach no less; they need nothing so much as the nothing-knowing of Taoist stupidity, for they suffer from cleverness in aggravated degrees. For who but exceptionally clever men could persuade themselves, for example, that supplying advanced weapons in large quantities to almost all the contesting powers in the Middle East would decrease the likelihood of the use of weapons there? A stupid man, seeing more weapons, would see only more·wars. And what but advanced cleverness would make officers of government believe that threats of war are the best way to prevent war? A stupid man, hearing dogs bark, would guess that they were likely to bite. He is not up to complicated methods of getting peace out of bellicosity.

Perhaps no aspect of life in the U.S. has been recently afflicted with greater cleverness than the economic aspect, and certainly no topic has occasioned a greater outpouring of knowledge than inflation. The last five federal administrations, Republican and Democrat alike, have dealt with it by restricting money and credit, even expressing hope for a beneficent recession and undertaking to limit help to the poor: first to obey the ritualism of holding government costs responsible for economic ills and, latterly, to encourage investment.

The cleverness of such programs is shown by the many economic complications their authors are able to rationalize away, such as decreasing industrial productivity and decreasing interest in productivity, increasing industrial mergers and increasing interest in mergers, together with the impact of skyrocketed fuel costs and high interest rates on costs and prices. The clever man masters the complexities of an economic situation and resolves them in an overall conclusion that is intended to mold the economy. The stupid man, by contrast, does not try to understand the situation but tries simply to look at the facts that compose it, trusting that later on the facts will themselves prompt the decision least likely to be' objectionable. Lao Tzǔ says:

> Many words exhaust Truth.
> Keep to the empty center!

For Tao, the empty center is also the center of man's multiform personality, with its unfathomable ability to explore unconsciously whole fields of activity that the conscious mind overlooks, and to let courses of action emerge through rumination about facts rather than through conceptualization of them. Indeed, there is a different way to look at reality from the conventional way we hold to be the only way.

As method, economics may be less reliable than a guessing game, which benefits at least from randomness. Its pretensions to science, logic, and mathematics (now that the computer is upon us) make it possible to talk up proposals that appear suicidal to anyone of no more than average stupidity. Influential economists are quite able to explain away such matters as the revolutionary change-over of an economy based on low-cost fuel and low-cost money to one based on high-cost fuel and high-cost money, the latter in the form of the interest rates that recently overwhelmed the automobile, construction, and savings-bank industries. Such changes, the stupid man might suspect, are likely to produce extremes of inflation and prostration, but the clever man has developed a mental grid through which he examines what is going on and by means of which he rejects what does not fit the grid. How else could he support the adage, which rose to popularity during the 1920's, that the cause of inflation is simply and exclusively the high cost of government?

Only a few decades ago, there were said to be not more than a dozen individuals in the country able to discuss such topics as the cost of money, the flow of money, and what might be called the equation of money. When these individuals talked, most bankers and economists took leave. The topics were held to be too complicated for general discussion. Indeed, the equation of money is influenced literally by everything that happens in the world, including what is said to be a part of economics and a very great deal of what is said to be no part of it. Included, in particular, are psychological factors, conventionally dismissed as undeterminable. Money can be said to move in the manner of a mobile of gigantic complexity, all of whose innumerable units can be put into varying and unexpected rates of motion by the simple touching of one very small and very distant unit. Money experts used to wait months and even years, watching not for the right answers to give but for the right questions to ask, playing in this way the wait-and-see game of stupidity. Nowadays, however, clever bureaucrats and economists have pontificated hopes for a recession which would, they dogmatized, cure the nation's ills, and they did not stop talking until the recession actually arrived.

The clever answer to the productivity problems was to divert money into investment. But the problems date not from some suppositious time when investment capital started to dry up, but rather from an actual time some twenty-five years ago when investors began to develop an appetite for quick profits from mergers, acquisitions, and conglomerates in preference to the slow profits that accrue from funding higher output at lower prices. Forgotten was the phenomenal outpouring of goods during World War II and the immediate post-war periods, along with the dedication to public service developed during those times.

Concentration on productivity to the degree of preoccupation with it was widely understood to be the only way to carry so wasteful an operation as world war. But peace, too, has operations of incredible waste, in addition to wars that are less than total and preparations for wars that may be total. The productive operations of the U.S. economy have to carry drone operations of enormous bulk that are always weighing the economy down; e.g., the operations of the unneeded goods sector of the economy, the useless services sector, the theft and chicanery sector, and also those sectors that support law and order in the form of the legal, penal, and military systems. The portion of the country's economic effort used up in attempts to curb wrongdoing is alone enormous, and — like other drone operations — it always tends to unbalance the economy. But it is also beyond critical discussion in public.

Many economic problems may be beyond discussion. At any given time in any given culture, people probably do not really know what their basic economic problems are. Otherwise they would be easier to solve. It strikes moderners as obvious that the economic problems of feudalistic Japan resulted from an imbalance, as Sir George Sansom was among the first to point out, between the numbers of the aristocrats, which increased polygamously, and the number of farmers who grew rice to feed them. But no one at the time was aware of this imbalance, even when a new social class came into existence in part as a result of it. Probably, the U.S. economy has problems of comparable importance of which we are similarly unaware, possibly as concerns effort lost in drone operations or wasted in supporting shibboleths about competition. Meanwhile there is always another Way, a way in which disaster is not the inescapable consequence of ignorance:

> The lesson of nothing-speaking
> The use of nothing-doing:
> Rare attainments beneath heaven!

For when experts fail, only nothing-knowing can succeed. A passive waiting for something to happen is transformed into an active force by simple awareness of the Way by which things happen whenever people are willing to let them. It is a way of getting outward results by inward stillness and sureness. It is a way of insight, a way of bearing the confusions of life until answers to problems work their way to the surface of consciousness. The contrary way of outward knowledge, of identifying the causes of problems, of assembling pertinent facts, and of drawing logical conclusions, appears to be a way out of confusion. But it is no way out at all, since what is causal, what is pertinent, and what is logical are questions too intricate for human untangling, whenever there is more involved than simple objects and numbers. Why not welcome confusion? Why let it lead to frustration and then solidify into neurosis? Confusion is a natural state of being from which, whenever it is comfortably borne, meaning emerges.

Cleverness lacks meaning; it provides no more than ego-centric thrill. When meaning is absent, social dissolution starts to occur, and the ordinary activities of life become as if tinged with death. Yet when cleverness disappears, Tao remains. Tao is found whenever sought.

5. Nothing-Wanting

The Tao Teh Ching is purposefully non-sequential, carefully repetitive, and intentionally non-conclusive. It is not trying to get anywhere since it is there already. One saying comes after another, often repeating the other without following the precedences of logic. The book itself is an insight. Composed of many separate insights, its method, arrangement, and purpose are themselves insights. And they are all of one piece. Gandhi used to say that the three aspects of Truth, simplicity, and non-violence have only one aspect. Wholeness is the essence of nothing-doing, nothing-knowing, and nothing-wanting.

> Keep to simplicity,
> Grasp the primal,
> Reduce the self
> And curb desire.

Lao Tzŭ's phrase for simplicity is nothing-wanting, which is neither an action nor a non-action but a state of being. And while he counsels against possession of people and things, he by no means counsels retreat from life and from other people in the guise of non-involvement and non-attachment. He counsels against self-involvement and self-attachment, and he decries anything that separates from the primal, anything that enlarges the self, anything that encourages the covetous. The counsel of nothing-wanting leads to simplicity whoever wants to get there.

> No calamity is greater
> Than not knowing what is enough,
> No fault worse than wanting too much.
> Whoever knows what is enough
> Has enough.

How does a person know what is enough? Certainly he does not discover such a limit by himself, even though it can be found only within himself. Something outside makes the inward discovery for him, and that outside something may be custom or it may be Tao; Tao as Tao or Tao as whatever term shall be used to indicate the source of meaningfulness in life. In times when custom is sloughing off, it is not until a person turns to the Way that he can simplify his life. And it may well be that he turns to Tao only because his life is so meaningless that it has become unbearably complex.

Indeed, the complexities of contemporary life are the inseparable consequence of lost purpose and forgotten meaning. Many people act as if they wanted to be forlorn, frustrated, and forsaken, as if they wished to live surrounded by an atmosphere of distress. In literature there is a marked absence of purpose outside self, and there are no longer generally accepted codes of behavior; there is not a commonly accepted body of learning, not enough even for literary allusions. Other arts reflect rootlessness, and painting so rejects the ways of nature that it fragments space and the beings occupying it. It seems to make little difference whether a man goes to church or lies abed of Sundays; he suffers from an absence of significance, and his centeredness on self does not rescue him from a paralysis of purpose. He feels the dull ache of aloneness, the swirling vacuity of frustration; and some sense informs him that that he is beset with deadness.

The misery of this deadness is too suffocating to bear. Besides, it is productive of exhausting tensions and angers when one miserable person confronts another miserable person. It therefore becomes a desperate imperative to find a way out of the deadness, and unless a true Way is found, it is easy to end up in one of a number of dead-end streets. Five of these dead-end escapes come at once to mind.

One escape is to cast off restraints on behavior in the conviction that, God having been overthrown, anything is permissible. Whether the anything is sex, success, or crime, it is made the occasion of sudden upsurges of excitement that reflect the hope that all life will be one long binge. Since life patently is no such picnic, this escape sooner or later closes up, usually sooner than later: it cannot survive the interruptions of daily existence or the interference of falling sick, getting old, and running short of money.

The second escape, probably the principal escape in the Bronze Age but not infrequent in an age of computers, is concentration on personal possessions and on the inward covetousness that spurs acquisition of them, leading to such common acts as addictive buying and compulsive self-decoration. This escape is a brittle one. "Do not," advises Lao Tzŭ," shine like jade or tinkle like stone chimes."

> Hold onto fullness?
> It is better to stop.
> Handle sharp edges?
> They can't long be kept.
>
> When gold and jade fill a house,
> No one can protect it.
> Pride in wealth and fame
> Breeds its own collapse.

In an age when there is little gold, not much jade, and no stone chimes, Lao Tzǔ's advice is often extended to material objects in general. His advice actually pertains not to the objects but to preoccupation with them. Some earnest people believe that having anything more than blue jeans, brown rice, new wine, and no heat is an obstacle to Truth so great that a search for it cannot even be started. This convenient excuse is one sometimes offered by people of high education and low income, whose possessions are typically not material but personal, consisting of their offspring, their spouses, and the more mentionable of their friends. But they wear the people around them with as much eclat as the rich wear fur coats and rare-metal watches. This sort of escape begins to fail when the decorations begin to talk back.

A third escape is a falling back willy-nilly on precisely those conventionalities in which one was brought up, perhaps under the illusion that whatever produced such a person as oneself must be life's true guide, a guide to how children should be raised or the house cleaned or the thermostat set. The attractiveness of this escape is usually blocked by hurt feelings and hard feelings when people nearby decline to follow the true guide, even when particularly directed to follow it. Moreover, the guide tends to exacerbate hard feelings towards the very persons who created the guide. Hatred chains many people to their parents more tightly than does affection, but they still feel dead.

A fourth escape is by way of compulsions, including obvious addiction to alcohol and drugs, more subtle habituation to selected neuroses, and hidden fascinations and intoxications of a sub-clinical sort. The insidiousness of such escapes lies in the illusion that compulsive dedication to particular things, activities, rituals, and emotions will clarify life out of confusion, simplify it out of complexity, and lift it out of inertness. A vain hope. People clamoring to be overawed by compulsions are usually overwhelmed by the inward racket they stir up, and the racket does not go away until the compulsion does. There is no chance of wanting nothing until an end is made of something-wanting. Wistful hopes for simplicity diminish as the complications of the addicted life increase.

Specific addiction to alcohol and drugs is recognized almost universally as a compulsive effort at escape, even though it often seems uncertain what is being escaped from. The victims of addiction themselves feel certain that they are escaping from something specific in the form of outside pressures and injustices, but the more they escape the more uncertain they are whether they are getting away from anything. Frustration ensues, and this mood can be changed only through more alcohol and drugs until all mood is obliterated in the vacancies of druggedness and drunkenness. For such addiction, the words of the Tao Teh Ching have a pertinence so obvious as to be amusing:

> Knowing what is enough avoids disgrace;
> Knowing when to stop secures from peril.

It is, of course, precisely the nature of compulsion that addicts are unable to know what or when to stop. They are powerless to get over their disease through any operation of their own minds and intelligence; the disease, indeed, has been called "self-will run riot." It is possible to recover from it by abandoning self-will along with the urge to know the why of addiction, a process undertaken in the mutual-aid groups of Alcoholics Anonymous whenever the addict becomes willing to surrender his will to that of a Power greater than himself, personified in the group, and to follow a new way of life. Will is traded in on recovery.

The compulsive character of the neuroses is self-evident to persons suffering from them, and these complaints have been successfully treated as if they were compulsions by encouraging surrender of self-will and discovery of a new way of life. But such treatment is new and relatively unknown. Only selected fears and cravings are usually named compulsive by psychotherapists. Treatment of the common conditions of fear, rage, depression, and guilt, together with the syndrome wherein all these conditions chase one another around in a circle, usually involves an understanding of the illness and an analysis of its causes, combined with a will to overcome the irrational by the rational. Relatively few patients, however, are lifted out of their afflictions by these devices, and in most cases the benefits of psychotherapy are palliative, resulting largely, perhaps, from ventilation with a concerned therapist or group. The mental health industry is as conventional as other industries, and nothing-wanting and nothing-knowing are not part of the business.

When compulsion operates on lower-than-clinical levels, it is seldom recognized as compulsion or as anything anyone ought to get over, for it is seen as nothing more than the inordinate pursuit of things commonly considered good in themselves, such as work, housecleaning, education, churchgoing, bookreading, woodworking, picturemaking, concertgoing, and gift-getting. Actually, there is little difference between chasing these in-themselves goods and seeking more dubious escapes in the thrills and violences of television or the artificial emotionalisms of the movies. When the pursuit of anything at all, whether good or bad, involves dependency on it, that thing plays the same role as the more obvious compulsions: it is pursued because it hides reality. Compulsion is inwardly more destructive than the objects pursued. The practices of churches can be as destructive as the tantrums of households. Immersion in hard work can be as overwhelming as immersion in drink. Reading literature can be as heady as shooting drugs. Prayer can be turned into self-worship. Only the Way itself allows of inordinate pursuit; the inordinate pursuit of anything else ends in destruction. Even the good of society. When it becomes a compulsion, it is as destructive to chase after it as status and riches and fame; and it is doubly destructive to be clever about it:

> When Tao is cast aside,
> Duty and humanity abide.

> When prudence and wit appear,
> Great hypocrites are here.

The illusory pursuit of compulsions or possessions is typically accompanied by ritual: that is, by a ceremonious repetitiveness that aims to give irrationalities and egocentrisms the appearance, if not of righteousness, at least of style. It occupies a place far down on a descending scale of aberrations. ("When morality is lost, there is ceremony. Now ceremony is the shell of loyalty and trust, and the beginning of confusion.") Even farther down the list is divination and the sundry forms of superstition:

> As to foreknowledge,
> It is a blossomy path
> And the beginning of folly.

The notion that nature can be magically manipulated to further personal interests is foreign to the Tao Teh Ching. In view of the association of later Taoism with magic and foretelling and the occult in general, it is well to emphasize that the Taoism of Lao Tzŭ is not less iconoclastic than other prophetic faiths. The I Ching, a work now popular among Westerners, reflects a mixture of wisdom and divination that characterized the Chou dynasty during which Lao Tzŭ lived, but its conventionality and superstition are not Tao but what Tao is against.

What of the religion of personal health, perhaps the only ancient form of faith left in Europe and America? A system of belief replete with rules of diets, lists of exercises, precepts about good potions and bad potions, and prohibitions of self-harming practices, it is shunned by Lao Tzŭ with the same vigor he shuns any other form of preoccupation with self. The Tao Teh Ching, in a comment about interfering with creation, describes as injurious a practice that much later became a popular system of self-fitness and self-spirituality:

> It is ominous to improve on life,
> Injurious to control breathing by the mind:
> Things overgrown fall into decay.
> This is not Tao
> And what is not Tao soon ends.

But, conversely, what is Tao never ends. Once the compulsions of something-doing, something-knowing, and something-wanting are cast aside, the Way opens. But that is the next chapter.

6. The Success of Failure

There is a general misapprehension that the Way of the prophets — of Isaiah, of Lao Tzŭ, of Gautama, of Jesus — is a very exalted way that can be followed only by very remarkable people, and that it requires a giving up of the normal activities and emotions of mankind and a rising up to heights of spirit which few human beings are capable of achieving. In the light of the teachings of the prophets, directed to ordinary people in ordinary walks of life, this misapprehension is nonsense. It is convention's effort to keep people under the dead hand of the past, to preserve at all costs the sway of violence and oppression and acquisitiveness and compulsion, and to prevent people from grasping the fact that they have only to become sick of their sickness to be set free from it. It is as if a man, seated on a stove that became hot, were to be informed that impossible fortitude would be required for him to get off it, when all that he needs is normal response to discomfort. Actually, it takes great fortitude to persist in old pain.

It is no different when people are sitting on their sick selves, for the emotional pain of chasing success and having unsuccessful run-ins with other people, of grasping knowledge and ending up possessed by possessions and compelled by compulsions: such pain can be as intense as any discomfort human beings can suffer. To get rid of the pain, nothing more is needed than a willingness to admit failure and to give up and get away. It then becomes possible to accept life rather than battle it, to simplify it rather than complicate it, to be open to it rather than understand it. The sententious notion that man must know himself is put aside, and an inward sense suggests that the self our society teaches people to seek is the self that it is impossible for a person to know. True knowledge is mutual rather than solitary, and the true self is not knowing but knowable. A man who looks into a mirror hardly recognizes himself and sometimes cowers before the strange image confronting him, but his friends know him unerringly at fifty paces and judge correctly the state of his mind from the tilt of his back. Such awareness proceeds from the true emptiness of Tao, an emptiness that liberates.

> Tao is empty! Use it
> And it isn't used up.
> Deep! It seems like
> The forebear of the ten thousand things.

It blunts edges, unties tangles,
Harmonizes lights, unites all dusts.
Existent and deep!
I don't know whose child it is.
It looks to be the source.

For once success has finally failed, Tao liberates. Truth liberates. The God of the prophets liberates. People come to realize that inward comfort and meaning are not to be found in what they try to make happen, but only in what actually happens. They find more. They find joy and awe, sometimes suffering but always awe and through the awe joy. Similarly people come to realize that they can find no comfort and meaning in self, that these are to be found only in the Way. And here they find the reward of failure: the stillness that is simplicity.

All men have plenty;
I alone am a loser,
A fool at heart indeed!
And stupid stupid!
The world's people are bright bright;
I alone am dull dull.
The world's people are smart, smart;
I alone am low low,
Bland as the sea, aimless as the wind.

All men have their uses;
I alone am stubborn and uncouth.
But I differ most from the others
In prizing food drawn from my Mother.

But these personal advantages can be found only socially. The Way can be followed — and prophetic faith in general can be experienced — only to the degree that an individual has life and being in a group. In the Bronze Age, there were at least remnants of the Golden Age to be observed in the lives of the common people and the barbarians, to whom Lao Tzŭ felt himself compelled to flee. In an age in which the remnants are principally those of a self-willfulness that still threatens the continuance of life, the way of learning the Way is by looking at it and walking along it together as a group of persons.

The Way is social also in the manner by which individuals can witness against violence and oppression. A group of people, inwardly concerned for peace rather than willful for outward success, can show the depth of their concern by taking trouble and suffering upon themselves (not, note well, by imposing trouble and suffering on others) and can in this way operate in the realm of spiritual reality, appealing to the deeper levels of being that people usually forget they possess. Thus did the followers of Gandhi appeal in their various campaigns against untouchability in India, showing their concern by standing for very long periods of time in an attitude of prayer. Such groups in effect renounce success since they realize that concerns of peace and freedom can prevail only when other people are inwardly stirred. The getting of publicity, the calling of epithets, the brandishing of signs, and the enacting of skits and burning of dummies produce no inward stirrings, which are the result not of cleverness but of example. To trust the Way that directs to peace is to trust its natural operations in the hearts of human beings once it is clearly shown to them. The Way the universe is constructed is the Way along which human beings sooner or later will come to walk. It is a Way not of justice or any other retribution. It is a Way of love.

> The sage has no fixed heart.
> He finds his heart
> In the hundred families' heart.
> He is good to the good;
> He is also good to the not-good,
> For virtue is good.
> He is faithful to the faithful;
> He is also faithful to the unfaithful,
> For virtue is faithful.

The Way, clearly, is the Way of the Kingdom of Heaven, but the kingdom is not simply at the end of the path; it is also the path itself. Truth may someday triumph totally, but the contribution of the billions of men and women and children to that triumph are small daily triumphs, and it is to these that Truth impels them. In history as in personal life, a very little bit of Tao goes a long way, and a turning to Tao that is hesitating and incomplete can mean life itself for a sick world and for sick people trying to keep alive in it. It can make all things new, and bring people to a new stillness and a new simplicity, so that they come to resemble the ancient masters:

> The ancient masters were
> Inwardly subtle and darkly perceptive.
> Their depth was beyond understanding.
> Because they were beyond understanding,
> They can be described only by appearance:
> Hesitant as if wading a river in winter,
> Reluctant as if fearing a neighbor,
> Reserved as if acting as guest,
> Effacing like ice starting to melt,
> Simple like uncarved wood,
> Open like a valley,
> Confused like muddy water.

> Who else could clear muddy water
> By quieting it?
> Who else could move clear water
> By bringing it to life?

For the changes in human affairs that take place in time result less from conscious planning and projecting, more from the inward yearnings of people's hearts, of all the people's hearts. The rulers can express themselves outwardly about the shape of the future, about how it should be arranged, whether it is to be peaceful or warlike, dynamic or static, but the future will take shape in terms not of how they express themselves but of how all the people live. In the light of the Way, problems arrange themselves if they are let do so. Lao Tzŭ advises, "Rule a big country as you would cook a small fish," a useful counsel of nothing-doing to a society that tends in its kitchens to dessicate meat and in its assembly halls to overcook life. There is only one Way to cook and one Way to live.

> From of old
> Its name has not ceased,
> For it has watched all beginnings.
> How can all beginnings be known?
> Inward light!

PART II

The Tao/Virtue Classic

Introduction

The Tao Teh Ching is addressed to all aspects of man, including that part which is as submerged as the bulk of an iceberg and measurably more immeasurable. For several millenia Asia's most read book, it has been frequently translated, but typically it has been addressed in translation to the visible part of Western man that passes for conscious reason. The habit of translators is to make the original understandable, to explain it. But how shall one attempt to explain a book that deals with the inexplicable? Lao Tzŭ is to be read with the eyes and felt in the belly with minimal interference from the reason. He is to be dipped into, lived with, perused again and again, but without regularity or purpose. His book is an invitation to insight not cogitation.

It is in the original stark, vivid, simple. To transfer its terseness and impact from ancient Chinese characters to modern English phonetics is to tamper with it, although attempt has been made to arrange the English words of the translation on the page in a way to hint at the feeling of the original. Simply to print the Tao Teh Ching in a phoneticised language is to do considerable violence to its original eloquence, which depends on look as much as on sound.

A scholarly translation of the Tao Teh Ching is somewhat contradictory in terms, but it is possible to aim at exactness. This translation has been much helped by the scholarship of Dr. John C.H. Wu *(Lao Tzŭ/ Tao Teh Ching,* New York, St. Johns's University Press, 1961) and by the effectiveness of his translation. (See notes, page 82.) The present translation tries to preserve the force, the rhythm, the repetitions, and the parallelisms of the original and even attempts a pun or two and an occasional rhyme. It declines to defer to the conceptual habits of Westerners by rendering such terms of Chinese concreteness as *the ten thousand things, the hundred families,* and *beneath heaven* into such abstractions as *all things, the people,* and *the world.* (It may be said that the finite is bigger than the infinite; somebody is more real than everybody; and the bounded is more extensive than the unbounded.) When, however, consistency would upset style, the shorter terms are used. The manner in which the Way is presented is also the Way.

While the translation seeks to be as exact in word as possible, exactness is impossible with a work of the spirit composed in the early morning of man's history, and some exactness of translation is possible only by recognizing that full exactness is not to be had. Generally, the translation tries to tamper least with the original terseness and impact. It makes no effort to explain the unexplainable, and it also avoids trying to make clear what is not clear, leaving unclear the unclear.

The absence of heads for chapters or other divisions in the original work makes for difficulties in the use of the Tao Teh Ching in translated form. There is no narrative, no progression of logic, not even connected argument in terms of which individual sentences, paragraphs, and chapters can be located. Persons to whom the Chinese language is native do not have as great difficulty locating passages as do Westerners, largely, I suspect, because early and long acquaintance with ideographic characters, which occupy space rather than define sound, trains memory of a visual sort to remarkable acuteness and makes it possible to locate quickly passages in most well-read texts. But this memory is seldom available to Westerners. Therefore, a key to first lines, which depends on sound as well as space, has been added to this translation. (See page 106.)

Notes have been appended to the translation in the thought that it is better to talk about the text than to try to make the text talk about itself. (The notes, which begin on page 82, bear numbers identical with those of the chapters to which they are appended. They are indicated by asterisks at the end of the chapters.) Their aim is to assist introduction to Lao Tzǔ through short sign-post statements, comments on textual problems, and brief quotations principally from Isaiah, Jesus, and the prophetic teachers of Quakerism and Hasidism. But it is the text which is to be read again and again — and without conscious attempt at comprehension. Scripture must dawn on the readers of it. Perhaps it would be wiser not to explain at all. The true scriptures, it has been remarked, are those which appear as blank pages, for words indeed fail when they are applied to that which is beyond words. But once the inevitability of such failure is recognized, it is possible to let untruth instruct in Truth, in the same way that noise instructs in silence. After all, Lao Tzǔ says that he who speaks does not know and he who knows does not speak, but he sets down a specific speaking for our instruction. Perhaps his book can be described as a joyful noise unto Tao that leads to true stillness.

The noise and stillness are pertinent to men and women everywhere, but it is important to remember that Lao Tzǔ addressed himself to rulers and their scholar-assistants, partly for the simple reason that they were the only persons in his times who knew how to read. The book sometimes sounds like a manual of topsy-turvy government, and indeed it has been used as such during occasional stretches of Chinese history. During longer stretches, it has been useful as a manual of non-government, but it is also a manual for marriage, for business, and for any situation in which persons meet persons and in which persons meet nature. In particular, it is a guide on how to remain whole in times of confusion. And it is constantly a book of hints on how to meet Tao. *

The Tao/Virtue Classic

1.

If Tao can be Taoed, it's not Tao.
If its name can be named, it's not its name.
Has no name: precedes heaven and earth;
Has a name: mother of ten thousand things.

For it is
Always dispassionate: see its inwardness;
Always passionate: see its outwardness.

The names are different but the source the same.
Call the sameness mystery:
Mystery of mystery, the door to inwardness. *

2.

When all beneath heaven know beauty as beauty,
There is not beauty.
When all know good as good,
There is not good.

For what is and what is not beget each other;
Difficult and easy complete each other;
Long and short show each other;
High and low place each other;
Noise and sound harmonize each other;
Before and behind follow each other.

Therefore the sage
Manages without doing,
Teaches without talking.
He does not shun the ten thousand things:
Rears them without owning them,
Works for them without claiming them,
Accomplishes but takes no credit.

Because he does not take credit,
It cannot be taken from him. *

3.

Don't exalt the worthy:
People then will not compete.
Don't prize rare goods:
People then will not steal.
Don't show what is convetable:
The people's hearts won't be upset.

Thus, when the sage rules,
He empties hearts
And fills bellies,
Weakens ambitions
And strengthens bones.

He leads the people
To not-know and not-want,
And the cunning ones to dare not do.
By doing nothing-doing, everything is set in order. *

4.

Tao is empty! Use it
And it isn't used up.
Deep! It seems like
The forebear of the ten thousand things.
It blunts edges,
Unties tangles,
Harmonizes lights,
Unites all dusts.
Existent and deep!
I don't know whose child it is.
It looks to be the source. *

5.

Heaven-and-earth is not humane:
It treats the ten thousand things like straw dogs.
The sage is not humane:
He treats the hundred families like straw dogs.

Heaven-and-earth and all between
Is like a bellows:
Empty but never used up.
The more it moves,
The more comes out of it.

Many words exhaust truth.
Keep to the empty center. *

6.

The spirit of low places does not die.
Call its mysteriousness feminine.
The gate of this mysteriousness
Is the source of heaven-and-earth.
Unceasingly, unceasingly, it seems to persist.
Use it and it won't wear out. *

7.

Heaven abides; earth lasts.
They last and abide
By not living for themselves.
Hence they live forever.

Therefore the sage
Puts himself last,
Finds himself first;
Abandons his self,
Preserves his self.
Is it not because he has no self
That he is able to realize his self? *

8.

True goodness is like water;
Water benefits the ten thousand things
But does not compete with them.
It stays in places disliked by man,
Therefore comes close to Tao.

For a dwelling keep to the ground.
In your heart keep to the deeps.

In dealing with others, keep to gentleness.
In speaking, keep to truth.
In governing, keep to order.
In business, keep to efficiency.
In making moves, keep the right pace.

If you do not compete,
You will not be faulted.

9.

Hold onto fullness?
It's better to stop.
Handle sharp edges?
They can't long be kept.

When gold and jade fill a house,
No one can protect it.
Pride in wealth and fame
Breeds its own collapse.

Do your work, retire:
This is the Tao of heaven. *

10.

In maintaining the vital spirit,
Can you hold to oneness
And not come apart?
In developing the vital senses,
Can you be like an infant child?
In clearing the inward vision,
Can you be without guilt?
In loving the people and ruling the state,
Can you hold to nothing-knowing?
In opening and closing heaven's gate,
Can you act like a mother bird?
While seeing clearly in the four directions,
Can you hold to nothing-doing?

Rear the people,
Feed the people.
Rear them but don't own them.
Work but don't claim;

Lead but don't butcher.
Call this inward virtue. *

11.

Thirty spokes share one hub;
In emptiness lies the wheel's utility.
Kneading clay makes a pot;
In emptiness lies the pot's utility.
Cutting doors and windows makes a room.
In emptiness lies the room's utility.

Gain can be had from somethingness ,
But use can be had from nothingness. *

12.

The five colors blind the eye.
The five notes deafen the ear.
The five flavors dull the taste.
Racing and hunting madden the heart.
Rare goods make men falter.

Therefore the sage
Tends to the belly not the eye.
He rejects the outward,
Clasps the inward. *

13.

Favor and disgrace: same fear.
Honor and distress: same self.

What is meant by
"Favor and disgrace: same fear"?
Favor makes the lowly
Fearful when they get it,
Fearful when they lose it.
That's why favor and disgrace are the same fear.

What is meant by
"Honor and distress: same self"?
The self registers our distress:

If we have no self,
We have no distress.

Therefore,
He who values all things as his self
Is fit to manage all things.
He who loves all things as his self
Is fit to be trusted with all things. *

14.

Look at it; you can't see it:
Call it shapeless.
Listen to it; you can't hear it:
Call it soundless.
Grasp at it; you can't hold it:
Call it bodiless.

These three are beyond scrutiny;
Therefore they blend into one.

Its upper side is not bright,
Its lower side not dark.
Continually the can't-be-named goes on
And comes back to nothingness.
Call it the formless form,
The imageless image,
The obscure.

From in front, you don't see its head.
From behind, you don't see its back.
But hold onto the Tao of old
And you can handle today's nowness.
Knowing the primal is the key to Tao.

15.

The ancient masters were
Inwardly subtle and darkly perceptive.
Their depth was beyond understanding.

Because they were beyond understanding,
They can be described only by appearance:
Hesitant as if wading a river in winter,

Reluctant as if fearing a ñeighbor,
Reserved as if acting as guest,
Effacing like ice starting to melt,
Simple like uncarved wood,
Open like a valley,
Confused like muddy water.

Who else could clear muddy water
By quieting it?
Who else could move clear water
By bringing it to life?

Whoever keeps to Tao
Does not want to be full.
Not full, he can practice
Concealment instead of accomplishment.

16.

Attain utmost emptiness;
Hold firm to stillness.
The ten thousand things stir about;
I only watch for their going back.
Things flourish,
But each returns to its root.
Returning to the root is peace.
And peace is a going back to reality.

To go back to reality is to be constant.
To know the constant is to find insight;
Not to know the constant is to court calamity.

To know the constant is to be broad.
To be broad is to be just.
To be just is to be manly.
To be manly is to be heavenly.
To be heavenly is to find Tao.
To find Tao is to live forever
And to rob danger from death. *

17.

Of the best ruler,
The people only know he exists.

Next comes one they love and praise.
Next comes one they fear.
Next comes one they abhor.
When you are lacking in trust,
Others have no trust in you.
Of the work of one who is short with his words,
The hundred families say, We have done it ourselves! *

18.

When Tao is cast aside,
Duty and humanity abide.
When prudence and wit appear,
Great hypocrites are here.

When the six relations have no point,
Filial piety and paternal love are taught.
When the countryside is out of joint,
Loyalty and allegience are man's lot. *

19.

Give up wisdom, abandon knowledge,
And the people will benefit a hundredfold.
Give up benevolence, abandon righteousness,
And the people will go back to natural affection.
Give up cunning, abandon gain,
And robbers and thieves will disappear.

These external rules are not enough.
Hold to what can be counted on:
Keep to simplicity,
Grasp the primal,
Reduce the self,
And curb desire. *

20.

Give up learning:
You will have no anxieties.
How much difference is there
Between ah and oh?
How much difference is there

Between good and evil?
What men fear
Must I fear?
Utter nonsense!

All men are happy happy,
As if consuming sacrificial feasts,
As if mounting the Spring Terrace.
I alone am mild
Like one who gives no sign,
Like an infant who does not smile,
Forlorn like one with no place to go.

All men have plenty;
I alone am a loser,
A fool at heart indeed!
And muddled muddled!
The world's people are bright bright;
I alone am dull dull.
The world's people are smart, smart;
I alone am low low,
Bland as the sea,
Aimless as the wind.

All men have their uses;
I alone am stubborn and uncouth.
But I differ most from the others
In prizing food drawn from my Mother. *

21.

The nature of great virtue
is to follow Tao alone.
And Tao's style is elusive, evasive.
Evasive, elusive,
Yet within it is form.
Elusive, evasive,
Yet within it is substance,
Dark and dim,
Yet within it is vitality.
Its vitality is very real:
Within it is trust.

From of old
Its name has not ceased,

For it has watched all beginnings.
How can all beginnings be known?
Inward light! *

22.

Twist and get whole.
Bend and get straight.
Be empty and get filled.
Be worn and get renewed.
Have little: get much.
Have much: get baffled.

Therefore the sage
Holds to the One and
Becomes beneath-heaven's model.
He does not show himself,
Hence he shines.
Does not assert himself,
Hence he is seen.
Does not boast his merits,
Hence he gets credit.
Does not vaunt himself,
Hence he survives.
Does not compete with anyone,
Hence no one beneath heaven
Can compete with him.

The old saying,
The twisted shall be made whole,
Is it not true?
Be whole and you will return. *

23.

Nature speaks little.
Squalls do not last the morning
Nor downpours the day.
What stirs them up?
Heaven-and-earth!

Even heaven-and-earth
Does not long make a fuss.
How much less should men!

Therefore,
He who follows Tao is one with Tao.
He who follows virtue is one with virtue.
He who courts loss is one with his losses.
Tao is glad to get whoever comes to Tao.
Virtue is glad to get whoever comes to virtue.
Loss is glad to get whoever comes to loss.

When you are lacking in trust,
Others have no trust in you.

24.

On tiptoe you don't stand.
Astride you don't walk.
Showing yourself, you don't shine.
Asserting yourself, you don't show.
Boasting yourself won't get you credit.
Vaunting yourself won't let you endure.

In Tao, these things are called
Tumors and dregs, which all things abhor.
Whoever has Tao does not dwell on them. *

25.

Something there is without form and complete,
Born before heaven and earth,
Solitary and vast,
Standing alone without change,
Everywhere pervading all things,
Mothering all beneath heaven.
I don't know its name;
I style it Tao,
And for want of a name call it great.

To be great is to go on.
To go on is to be far.
To be far is to return.
Therefore,
Tao is great.
Heaven is great.
Earth is great.
Man is great.

The universe has four greats,
And man is one of them.

Man follows earth;
Earth follows heaven;
Heaven follows Tao;
Tao follows itself. *

26.

The solid is the root of the light.
The still is the master of the restless.

Therefore,
The sage travels all day
But never leaves the baggage wagon.
Though there are arresting sights,
He does not stir but sits.

Why does a master of ten thousand chariots
Act lightly to all beneath heaven?
Lightness will uproot him,
Restlessness unman him.

27.

Good walkers leave no tracks;
Good speakers make no points;
Good reckoners use no counters.
Good lockers turn no keys,
Yet no one opens their locks.
Good binders tie no ropes,
Yet no one undoes their knots.

What is more,
The sage is always good at saving men:
No one is cast out.
He is also good at saving things:
No thing is cast out.
Call this following the light.

Hence good men teach the not good.
Not-good men are the lessons of the good.
Not to esteem the teacher,

Not to love the lesson,
Is to go astray despite great learning.
Call this the subtle secret. *

28.

Know the masculine;
Keep to the feminine.
Be beneath-heaven's ravine.
To be beneath-heaven's ravine
Is to stay with unceasing virtue
And return to infancy.

Know the white;
Keep to the black.
Be beneath-heaven's model.
To be beneath-heaven's model
Is to stay with unerring virtue
And return to the limitless.

Know the glorious;
Keep to disgrace.
Be beneath-heaven's valley.
To be beneath-heaven's valley
Is to stay with abundant virtue
And return to simplicity.

When simplicity diversifies
It produces instruments
That the sage uses as officers.
Indeed, a great leader does little cutting. *

29.

Does anyone want to take the world
And act on it?
I don't see how he can succeed.
The world is a sacred vessel
Not to be acted on.
Whoever acts on it spoils it;
Whoever grasps at it loses it.

Indeed, there is a time for
Some things to go forward

And some to go behind;
Some to blow hot
And some to blow cold,
Some to grow in strength
And some to decay;
Some to be up
And some to be down.

Therefore the sage
Eschews excesses, extremes, and extravagances. *

30.

He who uses Tao to guide rulers
Does not force beneath-heaven with arms.
Such things recoil on their users.

Where armies are
Briars and brambles grow.
Bad harvests follow big wars.
Be firm and that is all:
Dare not rely on force.
Be firm but not haughty,
Firm but not boastful,
Firm but not proud:
Firm when necessary,
Firm but non-violent.

Things that flourish
Fall into decay.
This is not-Tao,
And what is not-Tao soon ends. *

31.

Fine weapons are tools of ill fortune;
All things seem to hate them.
Whoever has Tao does not depend on them.

At home a gentleman favors the left;
In war he favors the right.
Since weapons are tools of ill fortune,
They are not tools for a gentleman,
Who uses them only from necessity.

Peace and quiet he upholds;
Victory he does not enjoy.
To enjoy victory is to like slaughter.
Whoever likes it
Cannot thrive beneath heaven.

Things of good omen favor the left;
Things of ill omen favor the right.
The under-general stands to the left;
The top-general stands to the right:
The way to stand at a burial rite.
Killing multitudes brings weeping and sorrow;
Treat victory like a funeral. *

32.

Tao is always without name,
Simple and small.
Beneath-heaven dares not subject it.
If kings and barons can hold to it,
The ten thousand things will pay homage.
Heaven and earth will mutually join
And sweet dew will fall.
Not by law but of themselves
The people will stay in balance.

When law and order arose,
Names appeared.
Aren't there enough already?
Is it not time to stop?
To know when to stop
Is to be free from danger.

Tao is to all beneath heaven
As rivers and seas are to rivulets and streams. *

33.

Whoever knows others has wisdom;
Whoever knows himself has insight.
Whoever conquers others has force;
Whoever conquers himself has strength.
Whoever knows he has enough has wealth.
Whoever perseveres has purpose.

60

Whoever keeps to one place endures.
Whoever dies without perishing lives long.

34.

The great Tao flows everywhere:
It can go to the right or the left.
The ten thousand things draw life from it,
And it does not deny them.

It completes its work
But takes no title.
It clothes and feeds the ten thousand things,
But does not own them.
You can call it small.
The ten thousand things return to it,
But it does not own them.
You can call it great.

Because it does not seek to be great,
Its greatness is accomplished. *

35.

Hold to the great symbol:
All beneath heaven will follow,
Follow without harm,
Quiet, even, secure.

Music and dainties
Make passing guests pause.
But Tao is bland and without taste.
Looked at, it can't be seen;
Listened to, it can't be heard;
Used, it can't be used up. *

36.

What is going to shrink has first been stretched.
What is going to weaken has first been made strong.
What is going to be ruined has first been raised up.
What is going to be taken away has first been given.

Call this the subtle truth:
The soft and weak conquer the hard and strong.

Fish should not leave the depths;
Neither should weapons of state ever be aired.

37.

Tao never does anything,
And everything gets done.
If rulers can keep to it,
The ten thousand things will change of themselves.

Changed, things may start to stir.
Quiet them with the namelessly simple,
Which alone will bring no-desire.
No-desire: then there is peace,
And beneath-heaven will settle down of itself.

38.

High virtue is not virtuous;
Therefore it has virtue.
Low virtue is always virtuous;
Therefore it has no virtue.
High virtue does nothing
And has no ulterior ends.
Low virtue does something,
Also has ulterior ends.

High humanity has no ulterior ends,
But it does something.
High morality does something,
Also has ulterior ends.
High ceremony does something,
And when it gets no response
It rolls up its sleeves and takes to force.

When Tao is lost, there is virtue.
When virtue is lost, there is humaneness.
When humaneness is lost, there is morality.
When morality is lost there is ceremony.
Now ceremony is the shell
Of loyalty and trust

And the beginning of befuddlement.
As to foreknowledge,
It is a blossomy path
And the beginning of folly.

Therefore,
The fulfilled man holds to
The solid rather than the shell,
The fruit rather than the blossom.
He avoids the outward, accepts the inward. *

39.

From of old, there are those who reached oneness:
Heaven reached oneness and became clear;
Earth reached oneness and became tranquil;
The spirits reached oneness and became mystic;
The valleys reached oneness and became full;
The ten thousand things reached oneness and became potent;
Barons and kings reached oneness and became sovereign.
Did they not all become so through oneness?

If heaven were not clear,
It probably would crack,
If earth were not tranquil,
It probably would quake.
If spirits were not mystic,
They probably would desist.
If the valleys were not full,
They probably would die out.
If the ten thousand things were not potent,
They probably would die off.
If barons and kings were not sovereign,
They probably would fall.

Indeed,
The great has its roots in the humble;
The high has its foundations upon the low.
Barons and kings call themselves
The orphaned, the lonely, the unworthy:
Do they not have their roots in the humble?

Truly, the parts of a cart are not the cart.
Do not shine like jade
Or sound like stone chimes.

40.

Returning is the motion of Tao;
Softness is the utility of Tao.
All things in heaven and earth
Are born of being;
Being is born of non-being. *

41.

When a superior man hears about Tao,
He goes after it diligently.
When an average man hears about Tao,
He both gets it and loses it.
When an inferior man hears about Tao,
He laughs loudly at it.
If he did not laugh,
It would not be Tao.

There is an old saying:
The bright way looks dark;
The forward way looks backward;
The smooth way looks rough;
High virtue looks low;
Great whiteness looks defiled.
Broad virtue looks deficient;
Solid virtue looks illicit;
Simple virtue looks decayed.

Great space has no corners.
Great talent ripens late.
Great music is out of key.
The great symbol is out of shape.

Tao is without name and hidden.
Hence Tao helps and completes.

42.

Tao bore one, one bore two, two bore three;
Three bore the ten thousand things.
The ten thousand things carry yin and embrace yang,
Whose blending breaths make them harmonize.

64

Men hate to be
Orphaned, lowly, unworthy,
Yet barons and kings
Use these names as titles.
Indeed,
You may gain by losing,
And you may lose by gaining.

What others have taught, I also teach:
Men of violence come to death by violence.
Whoever said this is my teacher. *

43.

The softest things beneath heaven
Overcome the hardest.
Nothingness alone penetrates no-space.
Hence I know the use
Of nothing-doing.

The lesson of nothing-speaking,
The use of nothing-doing:
Rare attainments beneath heaven! *

44.

Name and self,
Which is dearer?
Self and wealth,
Which is nearer?
Gain and loss,
Which brings more fear?
For:
Attachment comes at wasteful cost;
Hoarding leads to certain loss;
Knowing what is enough avoids disgrace;
Knowing when to stop secures from peril.
Only thus can you long last. *

45.

What is most perfect seems imperfect,
But using it doesn't use it up.

What is most full seems empty,
But using it doesn't wear it down.

Great straightness seems crooked;
Great skill seems clumsy;
Great eloquence seems hesitant.
Movement conquers cold,
But stillness conquers heat.
Clearness and serenity
Are beneath-heaven's norm.

46.

When beneath-heaven has Tao,
Race horses are used to haul dung.
When beneath-heaven has no Tao,
War horses breed in the countryside.

No calamity is greater
Than not knowing what is enough.
No fault worse than wanting too much.
Whoever knows what is enough
Has enough. *

47.

Without going out of the door
You can know beneath-heaven.
Without looking out of the window
You can see heaven's way.
The farther you go,
The less you know.

Thus the sage
Knows without walking,
Sees without looking,
And does without doing. *

48.

To get learning, add to it daily.
To get Tao, subtract daily.
Subtract and subtract

Until you achieve nothing-doing.
Do nothing-doing
And everything will get done.

To win beneath-heaven
Always avoid fussing.
If fussing is not avoided,
Beneath-heaven is not won. *

49.

The sage has no fixed heart.
He finds his heart
In the hundred families' heart.
He is good to the good;
He is also good to the not-good,
For virtue is good.
He is faithful to the faithful;
He is also faithful to the unfaithful,
For virtue is faithful.

Living beneath heaven,
The sage deals shyly with beneath-heaven
And simplifies his heart.
The hundred families strain eyes and ears;
The sage acts the child to all of them. *

50.

Going out is life;
Coming back is death.
The companions of life are thirteen;
The companions of death are thirteen.
For people moving toward place of death,
There are also thirteen.
How is that?
Because they live life intently.

It is said that
He who preserves his life
Meets no tigers or wild buffaloes on the road,
Remains untouched by weapons in the wars.
In him, the wild buffalo
Finds no space for his horns,

The tiger no space for his claws,
The soldier no space for his blade.
How is this?
Because there is no place for death in him. *

51.

Tao gives them life;
Virtue nurses them;
Reality shapes them;
Circumstance completes them.
Thus the ten thousand things
All worship Tao and esteem virtue.
No one commands them
To worship Tao and esteem virtue.
They do so of themselves.

For Tao gives them life.
Virtue nurses them, raises them,
Nurtures them, shelters them,
Comforts them, feeds them,
And protects them.

Rear but don't own!
Work but don't claim!
Raise but don't butcher!
This is called inward virtue.

52.

Beneath-heaven has a beginning:
The mother of beneath-heaven.
Knowing the mother,
We may know the children.
Knowing the children,
We may keep to the mother.
Death of body? No risk!

Block the passages,
Shut the doors:
End of life? No fuss!
Open the passages,
Meddle with things:
End of life? No help!

See the small: that is insight.
Keep to weakness: that is strength.
Use the light: go back to insight,
Keeping away from calamity
And practicing the changeless.

53.

If I have a grain of wisdom,
I walk along the great Tao
And only fear to stray.

The great Tao is easy indeed,
But the people choose by-paths.
The court is very resplendent;
Very weedy are the fields,
And the granaries very empty.
They wear gaudy clothes,
Carry sharp swords,
Exceed in eating and drinking,
Have riches more than they can use.
Call them robber-braggarts:
They are anti-Tao indeed! *

54.

What is well planted won't be uprooted;
What is well grasped won't slip away.
Sons and grandsons will keep the sacrifices.

Practice virtue in yourself:
Virtue becomes real.
Practice it in the family:
It becomes abundant.
Practice it in the county,
It becomes increased.
Practice it in the country,
It becomes prolific.
Practice it beneath heaven,
It becomes universal.

Thus persons are to be looked at as a person,
Families as a family,
Counties as a county,

Countries as a country,
Beneath-heaven as beneath-heaven.
How do I know about beneath-heaven?
Inward light! *

55.

One who is weighty in virtue
Resembles an infant child.
Poisonous insects don't sting him;
Wild beasts don't seize him;
Birds of prey don't strike him.
His bones are soft,
His sinews tender,
Yet his grip is strong.
He does not know
The union of male and female,
Yet his virility is evident,
His vitality perfect.
He cries and howls all day,
But does not get hoarse.
His harmony is perfect indeed!

To know harmony
Is to know the changeless.
To know the changeless
Is to have insight.

It is ominous to improve on life,
Injurious to control breathing by the mind:
Things overgrown fall into decay.
That is not-Tao,
And what is not-Tao soon ends. *

56.

He who speaks does not know.
He who knows does not speak.

Block the passages!
Shut the doors,
Blunt edges,
Untie tangles,
Harmonize lights,

Unite all dust.
Call this the original oneness.
It can't be had by courting,
Can't be had by shunning;
Can't be had by helping;
Can't be had by harming;
Can't be had by praising,
Can't be had by blaming:
For it is beneath-heaven's highest.

57.

Govern the country by regular rules;
Direct the army by cunning moves;
But win the world by avoiding fuss.
How do I know that this is so?
Inward light!

Beneath heaven,
The more rules and prohibitions there are,
The poorer the people become.
The sharper the weapons there are,
The greater the country's confusion.
The cleverer the people become,
The more cunning acts take place.
The more laws and orders there are,
The more thieves and robbers appear.

Therefore the sage says:
I do nothing,
And the people of themselves reform.
I love stillness,
And the people of themselves grow straight.
I don't fuss,
And the people of themselves get rich.
I don't want,
And the people of themselves grow simple. *

58.

When the law is dumb dumb,
The people are simple simple.
When the law is smart smart,
The people are broke broke.

Good fortune rests on bad fortune;
Bad fortune hides in good fortune.
Who knows the end of this?
It does not stop:
The normal turns into the odd;
The good turns into the weird.
Long have the people been in a stew!

Therefore the sage is
Severe, but he doesn't cut;
Exact, but he doesn't hurt;
Straight, but he doesn't strain;
Bright, but he doesn't dazzle. *

59.

In ruling people and serving heaven,
It is best to be sparing.
To be sparing is to yield quickly.
To yield quickly is to double-store virtue.
If virtue is double-stored,
Nothing can't be overcome.
When nothing can't be overcome,
No one can know his limits.
When no one knows his limits,
That one can take on the country.
When that one takes on
The mother of the country,
He can last and endure.

Call this having deep roots
And a strong stem:
Living, lasting,
And seeing into Tao. *

60.

Rule a big country
As you would cook a small fish.

When beneath-heaven is ruled with Tao,
Demons don't go spiriting.
Not only do the demons not spirit,
But the spirits don't harm people.

Not only do the spirits do no harm,
But the sage also does no harm.
Since both do no harm,
Virtue is restored intact. *

61.

A great country is one that downward flows
To be the confluence of all beneath heaven
And beneath-heaven's female.
For the feminine overcomes the masculine
By quietude and lowliness.

Hence,
By lowering itself before a small country,
A great country wins over a small country.
By lowering itself before a large country,
A small country wins over a large country.

The one wins by lowering itself,
The other by keeping itself lowered.
Great countries wish nothing more
Than to shelter others:
Small countries wish nothing more
Than to be sheltered.
Since each gets its wish,
The great country ought to make itself lower. *

62.

Tao is the refuge of the ten thousand things:
The treasure of the good man,
The backstop of the not-good man.
Fine words can be sold,
Noble deeds gain respect.
If a man is not good,
Why throw him away?

When an emperor is crowned
Or the three ministers appointed,
Discs of jade and teams of horses
Are not as gifts the equal
Of sitting still and offering Tao.

Why did the ancients prize Tao?
Because if it is sought, it is found;
Because the guilty are forgiven.
That is why it is beneath-heaven's treasure. *

63.

Do nothing-doing;
Manage nothing-managing;
Taste nothing-tasting.
Exalt the low;
Multiply the few;
Requite hatred with virtue.

Tackle the difficult when it is easy.
Handle the big when it is small.
Difficult things beneath heaven
Are made up of easy things.
Big things beneath heaven
Are made up of small things.
Thus the sage
Never deals with the great,
But accomplishes greatness.

Light promises indeed lack trust.
Much easiness leads to much difficulty.
Thus the sage
Holds everything difficult,
But meets no difficulty in the end.

64.

What is at rest is easy to hold.
What hasn't happened is easy to forestall.
What is brittle is easy to break.
What is minute is easy to scatter.
Deal with a thing before it exists;
Handle disorder before it occurs.

A tree of a full span's girth
Springs from a tiny sprout.
A nine-storey tower
Rises from a clod of earth.

A journey of a thousand miles
Starts from where your feet are.

Whoever acts spoils;
Whoever grasps loses.
The sage does nothing;
Therefore he spoils nothing.
He grasps nothing;
Therefore he loses nothing.

People often spoil things at the point of success:
Take it easy at the finish as well as the start;
Then nothing will be spoiled.

Therefore the sage
Desires to be desireless,
Does not prize rare goods,
Learns to unlearn his learning,
Returns the people to what they have lost,
Helps all things find their nature,
But dares not do.

65.

The ancients well versed in Tao
Did not enlighten the people
But kept them simple-minded.

Why are the people hard to govern?
Because they are too clever.
Clever government is a curse,
Non-clever government a blessing.
To know these two things
Is to follow the ancient pattern,
And to know the ancient pattern
Is original virtue.
Original virtue is far-reaching and deep.
It leads all things to return
Back to the great harmony.

66.

Rivers and seas become kings of the valleys
Because they lie lower:

That is why they become kings.
Hence the sage,
Wishing to be higher than the people,
Keeps his speech lower;
Wishing to lead the people,
Puts himself behind them.

For the sage
Stays above the people,
But they don't feel weight;
Stays in front,
But they don't feel hurt.
Thus, beneath-heaven
Gladly upholds him
And does not weary of him.
Because he does not compete,
Nobody beneath heaven can compete with him. *

67.

All beneath heaven say
My Tao seems like folly.
But it is great
Because it seems like folly.
Were it not like folly,
Long indeed would it have been petty.

I have three treasures,
Held close and guarded.
The first is love.
The second is simplicity.
The third is not-daring to be first beneath heaven.
Whoever is loving can be brave;
Whoever is simple can be generous;
Whoever is not-daring to be first beneath heaven
Can be a vessel of excellence.
But to be brave without being loving,
Generous without being simple,
Foremost without being hindmost,
This is to perish!

For love cannot fight without winning.
Cannot defend without strengthening.
When heaven helps,
It protects by loving. *

68.

A good soldier is not violent;
A good fighter has no wrath.
The best way to win over an enemy
Is not to contend with him.
The best way to use a man
Is to work under him.
Call this not-competing in virtue.
Call this using human strengths.
Call this mating with heaven as of old. *

69.

The strategists have a saying:
I dare not be a host,
But rather a guest;
Dare not advance an inch,
But rather retreat a foot.
This is called
Marching by not-marching,
Capturing by not-baring arms,
Charging by not attacking,
Seizing by not-bearing arms.

There is no evil heavier
Than to make light of an enemy.
To make light of an enemy
Is to lose what we value.
Thus, when armies clash
The one that grieves wins. *

70.

My words are very easy to know,
Very easy to follow;
But beneath-heaven can't know them,
Can't follow them.

My words have an ancestor;
My deeds have a lord.
People don't know him,
So they don't know me.
The fewer who know me,

The more honored I am.
The sage wears coarse clothing,
Inside himself hides jade. *

71.

To know and to be unknowing is best;
Not to know and to be knowing is sickness.
Only by being sick of our sickness
Are we not sick.
The sage is not sick.
He is sick of his sickness
And therefore not sick. *

72.

When people don't fear force,
Greater force is on the way.
Don't meddle with their homes
Or weary them at their work.
Only when they are not wearied.
Will they not weary you.

Therefore,
The sage knows himself,
But makes no show of himself.
Loves himself,
But does not exalt himself.
He rejects the outward,
Accepts the inward. *

73.

The brave in daring dies;
The brave in not-daring lives.
Of these two,
One helps, the other hurts.
Heaven may hate,
But who knows why?
This question stumps the sage.

It is the Tao of heaven
To conquer without competing,

To answer without speaking,
To attract without summoning,
To get results without hastening.
Vast is heaven's net and wide-meshed,
Yet nothing slips through.

74.

When people don't mind death,
Why threaten them with death?
If, afraid of death, they were still unruly,
Who would dare to seize and kill them?

The great executioner kills those who kill.
To take his place is like
Handling the hatchet for a master carpenter.
Whoever handles the hatchet for a master carpenter
Usually gets his hands cut. *

75.

When people are starving,
Their rulers are taxing them heavily.
That is why they are starving.
When people are hard to govern,
Their rulers are something-doing.
That is why they are hard to govern.
When people make light of death,
Their rulers make much of life.
That is why they make light of death.

Not interfering with life
Is better than glamorizing life. *

76.

A man lives soft and weak,
Dies hard and stiff.
The grass, the trees, the ten thousand things
Live soft and supple,
Die brittle and dry.
Hence
The hard and stiff

Are followers of death;
The soft and weak
Are followers of life.

For
When armies are stiff, they will lose;
When trees are stiff, they will fall.
The stiff and mighty will be cast down;
The soft and weak will be lifted up. *

77.

Heaven's Tao is like a stretched bow:
The top goes down and the bottom goes up.
What has much is shortened;
What has little is increased.

Heaven's Tao takes from those with much
And gives to those with little.
Man's way is not so:
It takes from those with little
And gives to those with much.

Who uses muchness
To serve beneath heaven?
Only he who has Tao!

Therefore the sage
Does but does not claim,
Completes his work but takes no credit.
He does not want his merit seen.

78.

Nothing beneath heaven
Is softer and weaker than water.
Nothing is better
To attack the hard and strong,
And nothing can take its place.

The weak overcome the strong;
The soft overcome the hard.
There is no one beneath heaven

Who doesn't know this,
And no one who practices it.

Therefore the sage says:
To bear the dirt of the country
Is to be master of the grain-shrines.
To bear the sins of the country
Is to be the lord of beneath-heaven.
Indeed, straight words seem crooked!

79.

When great ill-will is reconciled,
There remains ill-will.
How shall it be made good?

By the sage holding the left-hand tally
And laying no guilt on others.
If you have virtue, you do what you should;
If you have no virtue, you levy claims.
The Tao of heaven plays no favorites,
But it always succors the good. *

80.

Oh for a small country with few people!
There may be contrivances
In ten-fold or hundred-fold abundance,
But the people don't use them.
Let the people mind death
And not move away.
Though there are boats and carriages,
There is no occasion to ride them.
Though there are weapons and arms,
There is no occasion to show them.
Let the people again knot cords.
Let them enjoy their food,
Take pleasure in their clothes,
Find contentment in their houses,
And delight in their tasks.

Another country may be so near
That each hears the noise
Of the other's cocks and dogs,

But until the end of their days,
The two people never mingle. *

81.

True words are not nice;
Nice words are not true.
A good man does not argue;
An arguer is not good.
The wise are not learned;
The learned are not wise.

The sage does not hoard.
The more he does for others,
The more he has himself.
The more he gives,
The more he gets.

The Way of Heaven is
To benefit but not to harm.
The Way of the sage is
To work but not compete. *

NOTES

Introduction

The sixth century B.C. is the traditional date of Lao Tzŭ, but tradition has been widely attacked by practitioners of the higher and lower criticisms. The translator / prefers no-criticism and directs attention to a monograph by Dr. Hu Shih, "A Criticism of Some Recent Methods of Dating Lao Tzŭ," *Harvard Journal of Asiatic Studies*, December, 1937, an essay on the futility of something-doing scholarship.

The earliest surviving text of the Tao Teh Ching is that of Wang Pi, who lived in the third century A.D., but the earliest surviving manuscript of that text comes from the eighth century, about the time of the origins of printing in China. Thus more than a millenium of editing and amending took place before the book assumed its present form. In the manuscript of the eighth century, there are no divisions of any sort. The division into units known as chapters, undertaken in subsequent centuries, is entirely a matter of convention, and the division into paragraphs is according to the whim of commentators and translators. Traditionally, it has been assumed that the work falls into upper and lower parts, the former concentrating on Tao, the latter on Teh, or virtue.

The present translation results from forty-years' living with the Tao Teh Ching, from the guidance of the translator's friends, Dr. Hu Shih and Dr. Chou Li-fei, and from sitting down with dictionaries on one side and, on the other, the translations of Dr. John C.H. Wu and Dr. Lin Yutang, which the translator greatly admires and upon which he has drawn. The translation uses the Wang Pi text as amended in several particulars by Dr. Wu in his *Lao Tzŭ/Tao Teh Ching,* New York, St. John's University Press, 1961. The translator is particularly indebted to Dr. Wu, not only for textual scholarship but also for penetrating renderings into English of the Chinese original. Parts of Chapters 29, 39, 47, 56, 64, 72, and 78 use his wording. Thanks are extended to St. John's University Press for permission for this use. The Tao Teh Ching, in the words of the King James version of the Bible, must be "translated out of the original tongues, and with the former translations diligently compared and revised."

Sources for quotations in the notes are listed on page 105.

1.

Beyond words is Tao! The opening passage of the Tao Teh Ching has the vigor of the first sentence of the book of John: "In the beginning was the word, and the word was with God, and the Word was God." (John

1:1 KJV) The impact of the first lines is multiplied by an additional meaning: "If the path can be followed, it's not the path," and also by a derivative meaning: "If God gods it, he's not God."

In the original, the word *constant* modifies the second use of *Tao* in line one (and in line two the second use of *name*), but it has been omitted in translating because the impact of the rhythm of the sentences, as significant as their sense, is upset, and because the Western reader is not likely to imagine Tao as anything but the Absolute.

The phrase *ten thousand things* is usually rendered as *all things* and the phrase *heaven and earth* as *the universe*.

2.

Beyond opposites is Tao! Often assumed to be a statement of the relativity of values, this chapter is actually a song of praise to the beyond-everything wholeness of Tao. A turning *from* the relative enables the sage to accomplish but take no credit.

An eighteenth-century Hasidistic teacher, Yehiel Michal of Zlotchov, noted that "if there were no evil, there would be no good, for good is the counterpart of evil. Everlasting delight is no delight . . . the fact that evil confronts good gives man the possibility of victory" (*Tales*, p. 144).

Beneath heaven is typically translated as the *world*, a place of many meanings and a term of no location. *Therefore,* in classical Chinese, means simply that there is a link between what goes before and what comes after, but not that there is a causal or even sequential relationship. The logic of the Chinese language includes an indeterminism of intermingling happenings. In this translation, *for, hence, now, so, also,* and *thus* often substitute for *therefore*.

3.

Setting an example of contention is a typical occasion of contention. Quaker John Woolman wrote in the eighteenth century about "ways of living attended with unnecessary labor . . . which draw forth the minds of many people to seek after outward power and to strive for riches, which frequently introduce oppression and bring forth wars" (*Considerations of Pure Wisdom and Human Policy*, 1768).

Isaac Penington wrote about the value of not knowing: "Be still and wait for light and strength and desire not to know or comprehend . . ." (*Letters*, John Barclay edition, p. 173).

When the sage *empties hearts* and *fills bellies*, he meets needs but shuns covetousness. He also encourages humility. In Chinese, *empty-hearted* means *humble*.

The famous adage of *wei wu wei*, here translated as *doing nothing-doing*, is the positive form of *wu wei*, literally *not-do*, and thus signifies *do not-do*. Its full meaning, to be grasped only in context, embraces not only the wisdom of non-interference but also the forcefulness of taking action in the realm of the spirit: i.e., the realm of nothingness that is accessible only through humility. In this realm, humility is positive and passivity is dynamic.

4.

Apparently different in manner and meaning from Lao Tzŭ's hymn of praise is the hymn of praise of the later Isaiah:

> Who ever measured the waters in the hollow of his hand, |
>> or ruled the skies off with a span,
> or held the dust of earth inside a measure,
>> or weighed the mountains in a pair of scales,
>> the hills within a balance?
> Who ever moved the mind of the Eternal,
>> or gave him lessons and advice?
> Who ever was called in to give him counsel?
>> Who ever taught him how to act,
>> or showed him what to do?   (Isaiah 40: 12-14)

But differences in the outer clothing of words are swallowed up in the awesomeness of the Undefined, the Unknown, the Everpresent, whether that be the nameless JHVH or the nameless Tao. John Woolman writes:

> There is a principle which is pure, placed in the human mind, which in different places and ages hath had different names. It is, however, pure and proceeds from God. It is deep and inward, confined to no forms of religion nor excluded from any where the heart stands in perfect sincerity. In whomsoever this takes root and grows, of what nation soever, they become brethren in the best sense of the expression. Using ourselves to take ways which appear most easy to us, when inconsistent with that purity which is without beginning, we thereby set up a government of our own and deny obedience to him whose service is true liberty (*Considerations on the Keeping of Negroes*, Part II, 1762).

5.

How life-giving is the impartiality of heaven and earth! Treating all the people like straw dogs (that is, as objects of nominal worth that are burned in funeral rites) means treating all of them exactly alike, without regard for whether they are good or bad. The sage thus is encouraged to act in consonance with the One who causes his rain to fall on the just and the unjust.

Tao is sometimes conceptualized into a force, remote from human affairs, that acts as impersonally as the law of gravity, and this going-beyond-personality is true of Tao as it is true of the God of the prophets, but it is by no means the whole Truth. The whole Truth is Tao itself, whose breasts the sage sucks (see Chapter 20), and whose reality is known to man only through the human sensation of inward warmth that follows dethronement of self-will as the central force in the universe. In conceptual language, Tao is not less imminent than it is transcendent, but it is impossible to grasp Tao conceptually without losing it.

The hundred families is usually translated as *the people.*

6.

Only from low places is it possible to look upon heaven-and-earth. From high places, the temptation is to look down on earth and think oneself superior to it. Chinese landscape painters always lifted up their eyes unto the hills, never looked down from them.

7.

"The first shall be last and the last shall be first" (Matthew 19:30). "For whoever wants to save his life will lose it, and whoever loses his life . . . will find it" (Matthew 16:25). The danger is self. "Beware of striving in thy own will," wrote George Fox, founder of Quakerism. "Thy own will is deceit" (Epistle 97, 1655).

9.

"Seekest thou great things? Seek them not." So advises Jeremiah (Jeremiah 45:4 KJV). "Store up no treasures for yourselves on earth," advises Jesus, "where moth and rust corrode, where thieves break in and steal . . . for where your treasures lies, your heart will lie there also" (Matthew 6:19).

10.

Oneness. Throughout Lao Tzŭ, oneness, wholeness, the original, and the primal are terms that refer either to Tao or to the unspoiled condition that leads toward Tao.

"Can you act like a mother bird" is often translated for purposes of clarity as "Can you act the role of the female?" Lao Tzŭ is indeed persuaded of the superior role of the so-called inferior principle, but here he uses the striking image of *mother bird* and not the symbolic manifestation of *yin* in *yang-yin.*

Virtue is the reasonably acceptable translation of the second word of the title of the Tao Teh Ching, and it appears frequently throughout the text, in the course of which its meaning can be sensed.

11.

When the Hasidic teacher Aaron of Karlin was asked what he had learned from his teacher, he replied, "Nothing at all." He added, "The nothing-at-all is what I learned. I learned the meaning of nothingness. I learned that I am nothing at all, and that I am notwithstanding"

(*Tales,* pp. 198-199). Dov Baer of Mezritch says, "Nothing in the world can change from one thing into another unless it first turns into nothing: the primal state which no one can grasp because it is a force which precedes. creation" (*Tales,* p. 104). Of like experience is Isaac Penington: "[They] feel their own poverty and nothingness . . . Their way to become strong in Christ is first to become weak in themselves . . . self is of no reputation or value . . ." (*Letters,* 1796 edition, pp. 25 and 29).

12.

Outward excitements confuse inward experience. Early Quakers turned against music and art and dramatics, not for puritanical reasons but because these excitements played up and down on the emotions and made it difficult to attend inward Light. George Fox writes, "Whatsoever ye see yourselves addicted to, temptations, corruptions, uncleaness, &c . . . stand still in the light that shows them to you, and then strength comes from the Lord, and help. Then ye grow up in peace, and no trouble shall you move" (Epistle 19, 1652).

The last two lines of this chapter, translated literally, read: "Rejects that, clasps this." Throughout the Tao Teh Ching, *this* and *that* are used synonymously for inwardness and outwardness. Translations have necessarily an introductory character, and the choice has been made to render Lao Tzu's *this* and *that* with their closest English equivalents in meaning. As readers grow in familiarity with Lao Tzŭ, they may wish to substitute mentally the original terms.

13.

The difficulties of translating the first two lines of this chapter give some idea of the problem of language bridging. Literally, or as literally as they can be put down, these lines read: "Favor disgrace like fear. / Honor distress like body." Classical Chinese is as remarkable for the words it leaves out as for those it includes. Moreover, nouns are often verbs and verbs nouns. Making *favor* into a verb is one approach to translating the first line, but it requires additional words not suggested by the original. Dr. Lin Yutang treats all the principal words as nouns, and his translation reads: "Favor and disgrace cause one dismay. / What we value and what we fear are within our Self." Fortunately, the explanatory verbiage in this approach can be reduced, and the translation can echo the terseness of the original, thus: "Favor and disgrace: same fear. / Honor and distress: same self." The meaning is somewhat that of the popular adage, "Praise and blame are all the same."

Self, the last word in the second line, is a possibly dubious translation of *shen,* usually rendered as *body,* although it also means *person.* If the word *body* is used in this chapter, the chapter becomes somewhat impenetrable. But if the word *self* is used, the sense of the chapter takes shape instantly and dramatically. Dr. Lin uses *self* on the strength of a near-identical passage from Chuang Tzŭ, where the context makes the meaning evident. Dr. Lin's approach is followed here, but without full certainty as to whether the chapter means more than is evident in the original "body" of it.

16.

Returning. Lao Tzŭ calls repeatedly for a going back or a returning to the primal, the one, the Tao. Turning to the Eternal would be a close Biblical equivalent.

George Fox advises, "Return within and wait to hear the voice of the Lord there" (Epistle 5, 1652). And Francis Howgill, an enthusiast who died in prison in 1669, says, "Why gad you abroad? Return, return to him that is the first love and the first born of every creature, who is the light of the world. Return home to within, sweep your homes; you will see the leven that is there, the grain of mustard which the Kingdom of God is like, this you will see . . ." (*Works*, 1676. pp, 70-71).

Martin Buber writes, "It is known that turning stands in the center of the Hasidic conception of the way of man. But turning means here something much greater than repentance and acts of penance; it means that by a reversal of his whole being, a man who has been lost in the maze of selfishness, where he has always set himself as his goal, finds a way to God, that is, a way to the fulfillment of the particular task for which he, this particular man, has been destined by God . . . No soul has its object in itself, in its own salvation" (*The Way of Man*, pp. 25-26).

The second and third paragraphs of this chapter appear to be of a chain-argument character. See note to Chapter 59.

Man. In the line, "To be manly is to be heavenly," the character translated as *man* is usually translated as *king*, long its common meaning. But a few commentators have held that *man* was one of its ancient meanings.

Reality. In the line, "And peace is a going back to reality," the character translated as *reality* is usually translated as destiny. It can also mean *life. Reality* embraces both meanings.

17.

"If you do not trust, you will not be entrusted" (Isaiah 7:9, translated by Martin Buber, *Two Types*: p. 28). Isaiah's first emphasis is on being entrusted by the Eternal, whereas Lao Tzŭ's first emphasis is on being trusted by other men, but these meanings embrace one another so closely as to include one another. Both present the trusting relationship as a reality of creation and not as the whim of a man-resembling deity.

18.

We are not the dogs of God but his children. Prophetic religion has to do with relationships not observances, with awe not belief, with love not guilt, with life not property, with the Way not moralism. Obedience to the Way is indeed of great use if it is freely given, but of no use if it is compelled.

The term *six relations* refers to the relationships of father and son, older brother and younger brother, and husband and wife. The characters for *loyalty* and *allegiance* once meant *loyal ministers* and are sometimes so translated.

The liberties taken to produce rhyming lines involve no changes in meaning. In more literal translation, *are here* should read *abide, have no point* should read *are out of order, taught* should read *preached,* and *are man's lot* should read *abide.*

19.

On giving up righteousness, Hasidism provides a long and progressive history of treating the very piety to which it was wholeheartedly devoted as an obstacle to man's relationship with God and with man. "Being pious," said Pinhas of Koretz, "I prefer to being clever, but I prefer being good to being clever and to being pious." Several generations later, a teacher from the school of Karlin said, "Cleverness without heart is nothing; pious means false." In the sixth generation, Bunam of Pshysha said, "If someone is merely good, he is a debauched lover; if he is merely pious, he is a thief; if he is merely clever, he is a disbeliever" (*Hasidism,* pp. 166-167).

Martin Buber comments: "Whoever surrenders himself to a vague kind of love without accepting faith and wisdom will lose himself in bewilderment like one debauched. Whoever desires to confine himself to an emotional relationship to God without perceiving the living world around him robs mankind of what belongs to it. And he who is attached to God only by the external ties of traditional religion and morals, will soon lose even that weak hold which those external ties provide. Wholeness is reliable and leads man to God . . ." (*Hasidism,* pp. 167-168).

"What we must beware of is this persistent discrimination between ourselves and our neighbor, the conceit of discrimination, the deception of discrimination — indeed, this entire triumphal world of illusion, based upon a self-satisfying discrimination . . . The most extreme manifestation, in the scope of language, ever expounded in Hasidism against this overflow of false differentiation, is what Rabbi Raphael of Bershad said in the last summer before his death: 'We must now lay aside all pious deeds so that there will be no more estrangement . . .'" (*Hasidism,* pp. 181-182).

The first six lines of this chapter indicate the outward obstacles to the inwardness of the six lines that conclude the chapter.

20.

What men fear/Must I fear? In similar mood, Isaiah advises:

> Do not call out 'Danger!'
>> when this people calls out 'Danger!'
> Have no fear of what they fear;
>> never dread it.   (Isaiah 9:12)

A loser. A fool indeed! John Woolman writes, "I find that to be a fool as to worldly wisdom and commit my cause to God, not fearing to offend men who take offense at the simplicity of Truth, is the only way to remain unmoved at the sentiments of others" (*Journal*, 1756).

Stupid stupid, dull dull. It is said that "What is hidden from the wise and learned is revealed to the simple minded" (Matthew 12:25). Prophetic religion is of the people, not of the intelligentsia.

The meaning of *Spring Terrace* is no longer certain.

Prizing food taken from my mother. Mother refers, as it does throughout the Tao Teh Ching, to Tao. Tao is neuter as God is neuter, but Tao is feminine as God is masculine.

21.

Prophetic religions are religions of the Way. They call for a manner of living, not for a set of formal beliefs or prescribed actions, a manner that is grounded in the Way itself and open to its awesomeness. The book of Psalms reverberates with the cries of seekers: "Let me see thy ways, O thou Eternal, teach me what are thy paths" (Psalms 25:4). "Teach me what is thy way, O thou Eternal, and lead me by a level road" (Psalms 27:11). Martin Buber comments, "We may say that God wills that man should choose Him and not fall away from him, but we have to add that God also wills that His creation shall not be an end in itself, but a way; that His world shall be a way; and more than that: In order that this may be so in reality, He wills that his creatures shall go the way themselves, they must be in their own persons, from out of their own personalities. . ." (*Hasidism,* p. 109).

Quaker historian Rufus Jones says, "Quakerism at its birth was a fresh attempt to recover the *way of life* revealed in the New Testament, to reinterpret and re-live it in this present world. Its founders intended to revive apostolic Christianity. They did not intend to create a new sect" (Friends World Conference, 1937, Report of Commission).

Inward light! The original exclaims tersely, "By this!" (See note to Chapter 12.) The term used here and in Chapters 12, 54, and 57 is a phrase common among the early Quakers and described by George Fox, following the gospel of John, as the light which "hath enlightened every man that cometh into the world withal . . ." (*Journal*, 1648).

22.

How apposite are opposites! The tone of the first paragraph of this chapter is the tone of the later Isaiah:

> Every valley shall be exalted, and every mountain
> shall be made low: and the crooked shall be made
> straight, and the rough places plain. (Isaiah 40:14 KJV)

Moreover, in both tone and content, the first paragraph is remarkably similar to the beatitudes of the first gospel, which read as follows:

> Blessed are those who feel poor in spirit!
> the Realm of heaven is theirs.
> Blessed are the mourners!
> they will be consoled.
> Blessed are the humble!
> they will inherit the earth.
> Blessed are those who hunger and thirst for goodness!
> they will be satisfied.   (Matthew 5:3-8)

These observations, whether uttered by Jesus or Lao Tzŭ, have little to do with the precepts and strictures of conventional religion. What is described is not what will be or what ought to be but what, in the inward areas of men's being, indisputably is.

Between the themes of the second and third paragraphs of this chapter — between, that is, selflessness and wholeness — there is a clear inward connection. The twisted are made whole by reason of their giving up self-display and self-assertion. The whole to which they return is exemplified in a passage in Deuteronomy which Martin Buber translates as "Thou shalt be entire (undivided) with JHVH thy God" (Deuteronomy 18:13, *Two Types,* p. 61). To be entire is "to worship the Eternal your God with all your mind and all your heart" (Deuteronomy 10:12, Moffatt). To these words Leviticus adds, "Love your neighbor as one like yourself" (Leviticus 19:18, Buber: *Between Man and Man,* p. 51.) To Lao Tzŭ, however, love of God and man may be not so much the mark of wholeness as one of the characteristics of it.

24.

Pinhas of Koretz says, "What you pursue, you don't get. But what you allow to grow slowly in its own way, comes to you" (*Hasidism*, p. 129).

25.

In different words but in like mood is the later Isaiah's song of awe to the Eternal's creation, part of which reads:

> Can you not understand, cannot you see?
> Were you not told this from the first,
> have you not grasped this, since the world began? —
> that He sits over the round earth, so high
> that its inhabitants look like grasshoppers;
> he spreads the skies out like a curtain,
> and stretches them out like a tent . . .
> Come now! do you not understand,
> have you not heard,
> that the Eternal is an everlasting God?

> the maker of the world from end to end?
> He never faints, never is weary,
>   his insight is unsearchable;
> into the weary he puts power,
>   and adds new strength to the weak.   (Isaiah 40:21,19f)

The paragraphs from Lao Tzŭ, not less than the passages from Isaiah, are hymns of praise to the wonder of the creator and to the essential goodness of his creation. Unlike those faiths which view material creation as evil and which consider spiritual escape from it as good, the Tao Teh Ching is profoundly material and profoundly affirmative, considering good creation's every aspect: as does the first chapter of Genesis with its mighty refrain, "And God saw that it was good."

In the next-to-last paragraph, in which man is described as one of the four greats, the translator has again rendered as *man* a character usually rendered as *king*. (See note to Chapter 16.) In the last paragraph, the character used for *man* has always meant *man*.

27.

Paragraph one suggests that the way to solve problems is to avoid outward devices and clever plans. Paragraph two, however, seems to speak only of the obvious, something with little connection to either paragraph one or paragraph three. And the final paragraph is little more than Confucian in its conventional attachment to learning.

The temptation in reading scripture is to attribute anything out of key (or, indeed, anything less than excellent) to later additions and corruptions. This temptation probably should be resisted, simply because no one can know with certainty what is an addition or corruption and what is not. It may be wiser to disregard what fails to speak to one's condition than to attempt to rationalize it.

28.

Valley and *ravine* are words synonomous with lowliness. (They are also, as noted earlier, better places from which to view mountains than are high places.)

Infancy is considered to be a state of wholeness.

White and *black,* the shades of yin and yang, are symbols for the masculine and feminine.

Simplicity. This word can also be rendered as *uncarved wood,* a Taoist synonym for it, but the meaning of the final paragraph does not become notably clearer. If the first sentence is made to read, "When uncarved wood is broken up (or sawed up or cut up)," it seems to stand in apposition to the last sentence, "A great leader does little cutting." *Leader* can also be rendered as *cutter*, thereby producing a Taoist-sounding aphorism but without contributing more sense to the paragraph. See the final note to the preceding chapter.

29.

In the first paragraph, the common translation *world* is used instead of *beneath heaven.*

In the first line of the second paragraph, the phrase *There is a time for* does not appear in the text, but it has the blessing of commentators, of whom most were necessarily unaware of resemblances to Ecclesiastes 3.

The wondrously fulsome nouns of the final line are Dr. John Wu's.

30.

God is not out of this world! Neither is Tao! Lao Tzŭ does not propose any variety of beyond-creation ecstacy; he does not even mention anything similar to it, even though this device for serving self by getting out of everyday reality was probably as common in his times as it is in ours. The Tao Teh Ching is continually concerned with the mundane, with the social (in which Tao has to be followed), with, in this chapter, the hard realities of weapons and armies.

Looking at the Hasidic way, Martin Buber writes: "An immediate relation to God which does not embody an immediate relation to the world is self-deception if not deception; if you turn away from the world to turn to God, then you are not concentrating on the reality of God but merely on your own idea of Him. The religious element in isolation is not really the religious element" (*Hasidism,* p. 167).

Lao Tzŭ knows violence to be clearly not-Tao, "and what is not-Tao soon ends." In like manner, Isaiah knows violence to be clearly an offence against God:

> Your hands are full of bloodshed;
>   wash yourselves clean,
> banish your evil doings
>   from my sight,
> cease to do wrong,
>   learn to do right,
> make justice all your aim,
>   and put a check on violence.   (Isaiah 1:15-17)

31.

Whoever has Tao does not depend upon weapons; he uses them, says Lao Tzŭ, "only from necessity," but Lao Tzŭ appears to admit of his using them. In like manner, Isaiah has visions of a peaceable kingdom, but he does not interdict warfare in a land that is not yet peaceable. Consistency is not the problem here: consistency is the preoccupation of persons who wish to display the ideological purity of their own selves. Nor is the absence of specific planning for peace an issue: outward plans have a disturbing propensity for stirring conflict. The issue is whether there is a Way or a Realm upon which to depend, not simply for the partial, but for the ultimate conquest of violence and oppression. The issue is whether to have faith or not to have faith, to trust or not to trust in the Way creation is created. Isaiah and Lao Tzŭ trust. This early trust in the Way of peace remains the solid and lasting basis for all subsequent testimony against violence.

The *left-hand side* is the honorable side, the *right-hand side* the less honorable side.

The last paragraph of this chapter is generally considered a later addition, possibly in the form of a marginal gloss that crept into the text. There were no such military titles as under-general and top-general until the Han dynasty, which began in 202 B.C.

32.

No names! They are devices used by the human mind to get the better of creation by cogitating it and trying to explain it. They are devices used by oppressors to force life into molds and by the learned who put names to the molds. Tao is without name and is identifiable chiefly as a path. JHVH is without name, and is identifiable chiefly as a presence: the Everpresent who responded to Moses' question about identity, "I will be there."

There is not need for names if nature is accepted and not feared. Should it be feared? The gospel of Matthew reads:

> Look at the wild birds;
>   they sow not, they reap not;
>   they gather nothing in granaries,
>   and yet your heavenly Father feeds them . . . .
> Look how the lilies of the field grow;
>   they neither toil nor spin,
>   and yet, I tell you, even Solomon in all his
>   grandeur was never robed like one of them.
>   (Matthew 6:26, 28-29).

34.

Entirely different in word and entirely similar in tone is the cry of the Psalmist:

> Better a single day within thy courts
>   than a thousand days outside!
> I would rather sit at the threshold of God's house
>   than live in the tents of worldly men.   (Psalms 85:10).

35.

More attractive than the attractive is the simple. But not as visible and audible: listened to, it cannot be heard; looked at, it cannot be seen.

Jesus quotes Isaiah:

> You will hear and hear and never understand,
> you will see and see and never perceive. (Matthew 13:14)

Lao Tzŭ's outcry against learning has much to do with the desire of the clever to see more than eyes can simply see and hear more than ears can simply hear. Jesus, it may be recalled, praised God "for hiding all this from the wise and learned and revealing it to the simple-minded" (Matthew 11:25).

38.

The lowest level which the descending argument of this chapter reaches is that of foreknowledge. By this term, Lao Tzŭ appears to mean superstition of the self-willed sort that tries to fulfill personal desires. He does not mean that activity which Westerners associate with the prophets of Israel, and which the Tao Teh Ching closely resembles in inward character as distinct from outward language. It is well to recall that the *nabi* of Israel, the teachers who came to be called prophets, shared a marked distrust of the sort of prophecy that deals in prediction and roundly denounced the dealers. Probably they were the court prophets. Of them Isaiah wrote when he declared, "When they tell you to consult mediums and ghosts that cheep and gibber in low murmurs, ask them if a nation should not rather consult its God" (Isaiah 8:19).

Some generations later Ezekiel called out the word of God against the same crowd: "O Israel, your prophets are like jackals burrowing among the ruins! . . . my hand shall be against the prophets who see false visions and utter lying oracles" (Ezekiel 13:4, 13:9). The true prophets were persons who turned so wholly to Truth — to the Way of it and the Word of it — that they became intimate with it and sought to establish it as the ongoing force of daily life.

A blossomy path. In English usage *blossom* suggests hidden promise and inwardness, but in early Taoist usage it suggests fading and outwardness; note its use in the fourth line of the following paragraph and its parallelism with the third line.

40.

Returning is the motion of Tao. Isaac Penington writes, "But now I have been so tossed and tumbled, melted and new moulded, that I am changed into that which I thought it utterly impossible for me ever to be . . . In this state of folly, I find a new state of things arising in me" (*Pilgrimage,* 1650).

Being is born of non-being. Shortly before his death, Shneur Zalman of Ladi said, "All I can see is the divine nothingness which gives life to the world" (*Tales,* p. 271).

42.

One two three. Explanations of the meaning of these entities are sufficiently numerous to make it advisable to seek no explanation at all.

Gain by losing. This passage is reminiscent of Jesus' saying about losing one's life by saving it and saving one's life by losing it.

Death by violence. The saying of Jesus is that "all they that take to the sword shall perish by the sword" (Matthew 26:52 KJV).

43.

Nothingness alone penetrates no-space. Dov Baer of Mezritch says, "He who thinks nothing at all of himself and makes himself nothing, grows spiritual, and spirit does not occupy space." He says also, "You must cease to be aware of yourselves. You must be nothing but an ear which hears what the universe of the Word is constantly saying within you. The moment you start hearing what you yourself are saying, you must stop" (*Tales,* pp. 109, 107).

44.

Attachment comes at wasteful cost. Martin Buber speaks of "the lust for overrunning reality. Instead of making reality the starting point of his life . . . man submits to illusion, becomes intoxicated with it, surrenders his life to it . . . and he becomes all at once completely stimulated and in all his motive power crippled" (*Hasidism,* p. 39). This attachment obviously extends to possessions and intoxicants, but it also extends to those activities undertaken to prop up jerry-built edifices of self, such as great political and "religious" causes, which are often self-serving although speciously experienced as self-transforming.

Of late, non-attachment has become a popular phrase among Westerners since it suggests a rationalization for distrusting persons other than self and avoiding intimacy with them. Such rationalization, of course, is simply one more type of attachment to self.

46.

Knowing what is enough. Yehiel Mikhal of Zlotchov says, "My life was blessed in that I never needed anything until I had it" (*Tales,* p. 156).

John Woolman proposes that men and women mutually keep "to that spirit and power which . . . teaches us to be content with things really needful and to avoid all superfluities . . ." (*Journal,* 1759).

47.

The farther you go, the less you know. George Fox says, "There is a great danger too in traveling abroad in the world," and he advises a prompt return home (*Address to Friends in the Ministry,* 1667). Martin Buber writes, as if in explanation of Fox, "There is something that can be found only in one place. It is a great treasure, which may be called the fulfillment of existence. The place where this treasure can be found is the place where one stands" (*Way of Man,* p. 29).

The first six lines of this chapter follow Dr. Wu closely.

48.

Do nothing-doing and everything will get done. Proverbial in China, this saying reads in Chinese, *Wu wei erh wu pu wei*, literally, "Not act therefore no not-act." While there remained continuity in Chinese culture, it was the typical answer to difficult matters of government, ongoing problems of life, not to mention emergencies and catastrophes.

Nothing-doing includes, implicitly, nothing-projecting. Lao Tzŭ specifically rejects spatial projection (as in the preceding chapter on not going out of the door), but his rejection of temporal projection is only implied. Compare nothing-projecting with the sayings "take no thought for the morrow" and "there is no time but this present" (Matthew 6:34 KJV; Fox, Epistle 5).

49.

Goodness to the not-good. Inward recognition of Truth and the participation in it of all men constitute the pivotal elements of prophetic religion. Men of good will like Confucius hold that unkindness should be repaid with justice; otherwise, how should kindness be repaid? Men of prophetic inwardness, uninterested in notions of repayment, know that all men are one. Martin Buber, as already noted, translates Leviticus 19:18 as "You shall love your neighbor as one like yourself." (See Note to Chapter 20.) The Sermon on the Mount links common sonship, love of enemies, and the Way of creation with divine impartiality:·

> He makes his sun rise on the evil and the good,
> and sends rain on the just and the unjust.
>
> (Matthew 5:44-45)

In Luke's version, Jesus declares,

> Love your enemies, do good to those who hate you:
> bless those who curse you, pray for those who
> abuse you . . .
> you will be sons of the Most High —
> for he is kind even to the ungrateful and the evil.
>
> (Luke 6, 27-28, 35)

George Fox was sufficiently imbued with this prophetic spirit to forget on occasion even to mention the not-good, as when he advised Friends "to walk cheerfully around the world answering that of God in every man" and when he stressed "Doing Truth to all, without respect to persons; to high and low whatsoever, young or old, rich or poor" (*Journal*, 1656, p. 263; *Line of Righteousness,* 1661).

One of the Hasidic teachers says, "The real love of God should begin with the love of man. And if anyone should tell you that he has love of God but has no love of man, then know that he is lying."

(*Hasidism,* p. 168). According to the early Quakers, there is a divine light in every man. According to the early Hasidim, there is a divine particle in every man, and one, moreover, that is peculiar to him. Hence every man has divine worth. Yehiel-Michal of Zloczov says, "Pray for your enemies that all my be well with them. And should you think this is not serving God, rest assured that more than all prayers, this is, indeed, the service of God" (*Tales,* p. 156).

50.

The thirteen companions. It is not known what these were, and what has been suggested seems to add little sense to a paragraph that is somewhat lacking in it.

No space for death. Notwithstanding the complex imagery of this paragraph, Lao Tzŭ gives simple and repeated witness to immortality. See also Chapters 16 and 52.

53.

Robbers-braggarts. "What mean you," demands Isaiah, "by crushing my people and grinding the face of the poor?" (Isaiah 3:15). He is anguished by the rich: "their land so full of silver and gold, no end to their stores; their land so full of horses, no end to their war-chariots" (Isaiah 3:15, 2:17). The Epistle of James declares:

> Come now, you rich men, weep and shriek over
> your impending miseries!
> You have been storing up treasure in the very
> last days;
> your wealth lies rotting,
> and your clothes are moth-eaten;
> your gold and silver lie rusted over
> and their rust will be evidence against you . . .
> See the wages of which you have defrauded the
> workmen who mowed your fields call out . . .
> You have condemned, you have murdered the
> righteous — unresisting.   (James 5:1-6)

In the last two lines of Chapter 53, the text puns seriously on the words *robber* and *Tao,* which are pronounced alike. The gaudily clothed can be Tao-braggarts as well as robber-braggarts and, consequently, they can be against themselves as well as against Tao.

54.

The third line in the first paragraph on sacrifices is unlike Lao Tzŭ.

Inward light! The inwardness which Lao Tzŭ designated by the pronoun *this* is the Way by which we learn as well as the Way upon which we journey. This is, we follow light, and it is light that informs us both about the Way and about the Way to follow it. "And this," said George Fox after an experience of inward opening, "I knew experimentally" (*Journal,* 1647). Prophetic persons characteristically experience spiritual truths, of which inward light is one, as incontrovertible facts of experience. The Psalmist says:

> 'Tis inward truth that thou desirest;
> grant me then wisdom in my secret heart.　　(Psalms 51:6)

55.

An infant child. Return to infancy! Jesus says, "I tell you truly, unless you turn and become like children, you will never get into the Realm of heaven at all. Whoever humbles himself like this child, he is the greatest in the Realm of Heaven . . ." (Matthew 18:3-4).

Dov Baer of Mezritch says, "From the child you can learn three things: He is merry for no particular purpose; Never for a moment is he idle; When he needs something, he demands it vigorously" (*Tales*, p. 105).

Evident virility and *perfect vitality* are references to infant sexuality.

Control breathing. From this saying and from the comment on foreknowledge in Chapter 38, it may be assumed that practices that became associated with later Taoism and with the Buddhism later imported into China from India existed long before the times of Lao Tzǔ. To him, such practices were, of course, uncongenial; popular indifference to his teachings against them is one sign of how truly *unsuccessful* he was.

57.

Win the world by avoiding fuss. About 1660, George Fox advised Friends how Truth should be advanced in the world at large: "Let your conversation preach to all men and your innocent love . . . Live in the peaceable life, doing good to all men, and seeking the good and welfare of all men" (*Paper to Friends* etc., Swarthmore Manuscripts 7:46). He also urged Friends to "walk cheerfully over the world, answering that of God in everyone" (See note to Chapter 49).

Roughly a hundred years later, Israel of Rizhyn said, "If a man speaks in the spirit of truth and listens in the spirit of truth, one word is enough, for with one word can the world be uplifted, and with one word can the world be redeemed" (*Tales*, p. 236).

Martin Buber has written, "If we had power over the ends of the earth, it would not give us that fulfillment of existence which a quiet devoted relationship to nearby life can give us. If we knew the secrets of the upper worlds, they would not allow us so much actual participation in true existence as we can achieve by performing, with holy intent, a task belonging to our daily duties. Our treasure is hidden beneath the hearth of our own home" (*The Way of Man*, p. 30). What is done by being does more than what is done by doing.

58.

Long have the people been in a stew can be rendered less vulgarly as "Long have the people been astray."

59.

Chain argument. The entire argument of this chapter involves forging linkage from *being sparing* all the way up to *envisioning Tao*. The question is whether the links are philological rather than psychological in character: whether, that is, they are arbitrary rather than realistic, and thus concerned with name calling and the rectifying of terms, as in not a few other early Chinese writings, including a number of the Confucian classics. In the Tao Teh Ching, argument of a similar character is present in chapters 16, 38, and 67.

In the Tao Teh Ching, it should be noted, each of the coupled links represent aspects of actual life rather than philological consideration. Psychological fact is built upon psychological fact. This approach is not uncommon among prophetic writings of a realistic character, including some of recent appearance. In 1764, John Woolman wrote, "Doth pride lead to vanity? Doth vanity form imaginary wants? Do these wants prompt men to exert their power in requiring that of others which themselves would rather be excused from . . .? Do these proceedings beget hard thoughts? Do hard thoughts, when ripe, become malice? Does malice, when ripe, become revengeful, and in the end inflict terrible pains on their fellow-creatures and spread desolations in the world?" (*Journal,* 1764).

60.

Demons and spirits. It is as startling to come across, however briefly, aspects of superstition in the iconoclastic Tao Teh Ching as it would be to come upon a favorable mention of idols in the Book of Isaiah. The only possible meaning that can be extracted from this chapter, as we have it, is one taken by conventional people: if the government is in order, the demons and spirits are thereby rendered ineffective, a notion that has Confucian aspects but not Taoist ones. It can be argued, of course, and probably correctly that the text has been corrupted by glosses and rewritings, but this argument is of little use to persons who read scriptures as scripture and not as philological exercises.

The moment one argues that troublesome passages are corruptions, one attributes a subjectivity to the text that clouds the whole of it with unreality. To repeat, it may be better simply to note troublesome passages and then — unless they become clear later on — to put them off to one side as deficient in present pertinence.

61.

Winning by lowering. By the sixth century B.C. in China, war and violence were no longer occasional outbreaks but continuing upheavals.

The separate states that composed the Chou Empire fought among themselves and against Chou, weakened after some five centuries of rule. To have expected any country participating in this on-going strife suddenly to attempt victory by lowering itself would have been similar to expecting any of the nobles participating in the oppressions of the times suddenly to lower himself before the oppressed, who in those Bronze Age times were confined to Neolithic homes, utensils, and manner of living.

Did Lao Tzŭ tell a tale of Tao that would apply only out of time, out of space, and finally out of this world? When Isaiah, in an environment of comparable violence and oppression, expressed his vision of a peaceable kingdom, was he too projecting a future beyond reality? For he said, "Nation shall not lift up sword against nation, neither shall they learn war any more" (Isaiah 2:4 KJV). And what was Jesus projecting when he said, "Resist not evil"? (Matthew 5:39 KJV).

Ever since these teachings were uttered, the conventionally minded have sought to banish them from this life, at least. They are, however, part of the Way and that Way is not invalidated by the world's not having reached the destination of it. But with the possibility of atomic destruction there is a possibility of testing the teachings. If human life conquers over violence, it will be because teachers such as Isaiah, Lao Tzŭ, and Jesus envisioned long ago the possibility of men, women, and children realizing in historical time increasing evidences of the Truth by which they live in their daily undertakings. It will be because teachings of the Way have not been banished from the hearts of common ordinary men, including common ordinary conventionalists, for they are notably out of touch with their own hearts. The Realm of Truth, of God, of Tao comes into the world only through inward existence in the lives of those who commit themselves to it.

62.
   If it is sought it is found. The Gospel according to Matthew says:

> Ask and the gift will be yours,
>   seek and you will find,
>   knock and the door will open to you.   (Matthew 7:7)

66.
   Puts himself behind them. Luke records that:

> . . . everyone who uplifts himself will be humbled
> and he who humbles himself will be uplifted.   (Luke 18:16)

67.
   Translated as *love* is a character often translated as *mercy* or *pity* or *compassion.* The type of love referred to is that of a tender and maternal nature.

68.

Serve under. The injunction of Jesus reads:

> He who is greatest among you must be your servant.
> Whoever uplifts himself will be humbled,
>   and whoever humbles himself will be uplifted.
>
> (Matthew 23:11-12)

69.

Seizing by not-bearing arms. It is said in the book of Isaiah:

> Arm for the fray,
>   and you will be shattered! . . .
> Form your plot,
>   and it will fail.   (Isaiah 8:9-10)

Abraham, the Angel, says: "I have learned a new form of service from the wars of Frederick, King of Prussia. It is not necessary to approach the enemy in order to attack him. In fleeing from him, it is possible to circumvent him as he advances, and fall on him from the rear until he is forced to surrender. What is needed is not to strike straight at Evil, but to withdraw to the sources of divine power, and from there to circle around Evil, bend it, and transform it into its opposite" (*Tales,* p. 115). This statement could be a commentary on Chinese guerilla tactics.

Grieves can also be read as *yields.*

The first five lines of the chapter follow Dr. Wu exactly.

70.

Unpopular is the role of prophet. John Woolman says, "The messages of the prophet Jeremiah were so disagreeable to the people, and so reverse to the spirit they lived in, that he became the object of their reproach, and in the weakness of nature thought to desist from his prophetic office; but, saith he, *His word was in my heart as a burning fire shut up in my bones, and I was weary with forbearing and could not stay.* I saw at this time that if I was honest to declare that which Truth opened in me, I could not please all men . . . From one age to another, the gloom grows thicker and darker, till error gets established by general opinion, so that whoever attends to perfect goodness and remains under the melting influence of it, finds a path unknown to many and sees the necessity to lean upon the arm of divine strength and dwell alone or with a few in the right . . ." (*Journal,* 1756, 1759).

71.

The first two lines of this chapter are among the most difficult in the Tao Teh Ching to translate. Literally, they read: "Know not know best./Not know know sickness." All translators come up with different renderings, and the reader is invited to come up with his own, bearing in mind that extra words will have to be added and that verbs can interchange with nouns. Some translators treat the *knows* in the first two sentences as nouns, whence comes the following: "To treat knowledge as ignorance is best./To treat ignorance as knowledge is sickness." The present translation treats all the *knows* as verbal forms and tries to be terse.

72.

Does not exalt himself. John Woolman writes, "As death comes to our own wills and a new way of life is formed in us, the heart is purified and prepared to understand clearly . . ." (*Journal*, 1772). "When I silently ponder on that change that was wrought in me, I find no language equal to it, nor any means to convey to another a clear idea of it. I looked upon the works of God in this visible creation, and an awfulness covered me. My heart was tender and often contrite, and a universal love to my fellow creatures increased in me. This will be understood by such who have trodden in the same path" (*Journal*, 1760).

The first five lines of the second paragraph of Chapter 62 come verbatim from Dr. Wu's translation, which concludes, "He prefers what is within to what is without." The two-line conclusion is here retranslated to keep it as terse as possible.

74.

If they still feared death? Since Lao Tzŭ sees no trouble in death, why should he, in this chapter, write as if fear of death were something natural to the people that the better-off had deprived them of? Possibly, Lao Tzŭ was writing about that fear which is awe, awe of the sort that the prophets of Israel called for.

The great executioner. The word *great* is not in the text, but it is approved by numerous commentators and translators. *Master carpenter*, however, is *master carpenter*; the word *great* is part of the text.

75.

Taxing and *something-doing.* Isaiah declares:

> Woe to those who issue harsh decrees,
>   penning orders that oppress,
> robbing the weak of their rights,
>   and defrauding the poor of their dues,
> till widows fall to them as spoil
>   and orphans as their prey.
> What will you do at the great Assize,
>   when the storm blows from abroad?   (Isaiah 10:1-3)

Jesus cries out, "Woe to you rich folk" (Luke 6:24). John Woolman writes, "And here luxury and covetousness, with all the numerous oppressions and other evils attending them, appeared very afflicting to me; and I felt in that which is immutable that the seeds of great calamity and desolation are sown and growing on this continent" (*Journal*, 1763). "Thus oppression in the extreme appears terrible, but oppression in more refined appearances remains to be oppression; and where the smallest degree of it is cherished, it grows stronger and more extensive . . ." (*A Plea for the Poor*, 1793). "Do I, in all my proceedings, keep to that use of things which is agreeable to universal righteousness?" (Journal, 1761).

76.
   The weak. The Psalmist also declares that they fare well, saying, "Happy is he who remembers the weak and the poor" (Psalms 41:1). The Psalmist says also:

> For the Eternal saves the forlorn who cry to him,
>   the weak and the helpless;
> he pities the forlorn and weak,
>   he saves the life of the weak,
> rescuing them from outrage and oppression —
>   they are not cheap to him.   (Psalms 73:12-14)

79.
   The left-hand tally recorded debits, the *right-hand tally* credits.

80.
   Oh for a small country with few people, but we now live in very large countries with many people, and in a world that has suddenly become unimaginably populated, not simply in terms of the Bronze Age, but of all the centuries preceding this age of high technology. The vision of a small country, attractive in its simplicity, was one tenable in the Bronze Age, when it was still possible to witness Neolithic simplifications with one's own eyes, when the invention of bronze meant nothing better than the production of sacrificial vases and of weapons of war, when the invention of writing meant nothing better than divination and the recording of taxes.
   It is a vision shared by some moderns of prophetic temper, such as Thoreau and Gandhi. Persons like John Woolman have also noted that the more anyone had, the less there was for everyone else to have, but this relationship pertained to pre-industrial economies based on limited production and scarcity. The vision of visible smallness and of visually obvious interdependence is one whose inward feeling could be experienced only in unpopulated times. Be it remembered that Lao Tzŭ did not simply *knot cords* (the method of reckoning before the invention of writing): he wrote. His vision of isolation was not truly what he called a return; it was a backward look.
   Now the vision is gone. Were there to be substantially less machinery

and transportation in the world, billions of people would, in effect, be sentenced to death. To some social reformers, including some who have wished to deprive poor countries of insecticides so that they themselves would be free of the guilt of manufacturing them, this eventuality seems not to be of primary concern, but it must be primary to any person who senses the oneness of mankind. Men and women have not been created in such a way that they can seek spiritual reality in their own lives while looking upon, let alone condoning, the physical wasting and destruction of multitudes of their fellows. The reality behind Lao Tzŭ's vision can now be realized only in a world of many people.

Such a world is only slightly different, after all, from a world of a few people. It is possible to be simple in any circumstances; and it may be that the more trying circumstances are, the easier it is to become simple.

81.

Lao Tzŭ's final counsel is to keep away from niceness, to keep out of arguments, and to keep with simple factuality instead of cogitation's complex constructions: a useful counsel not only for making the most of life but also for finding the most in scripture. Upon finishing the reading of an unfamiliar scripture, the reader of modern habits finds it tempting to evaluate it, and thus to establish control over it by the processes of the intellect: a procedure not very different from some forms of stone-age superstition. Appreciate life, don't evaluate it; appreciate scripture, don't evaluate it. If it is worth reading, it is clearly beyond the evaluation of anyone, including the persons who wrote it, let alone beyond anyone's control. Comparisons will indeed come to mind. Lao Tzŭ, for example, may not seem to be as vehemently dialogical as the prophets of Israel. But comparisons should not be kept in mind. The Tao Teh Ching is differently dialogical, but who is to say whether or not it is equally dialogical? It is, among many things, one of the most remarkable prayers ever uttered or written, and to this prayer the whole Tao of creation gives dialogical answer.

True prophetic religions are not exclusive by their inward nature; they are supplemental. One scripture adds to the other, because one does not take the place of the older. Their similarities point to their common source: and the fact that they are so remarkably alike persuades not alone of their common but also of their individual truth. When new faith supplements old faith, it renews. But when new faith supplants old faith, it deadens. It is unproductive to look at a new scripture as if it were something for which to give up the scripture one has. It is nourishing to add the new to the old.

William Penn writes: "The humble, meek, merciful, just, pious and devout souls are everywhere of one religion; and when death has taken off the mask, they will know one another, though the divers liveries they wear here makes them strangers" (*Some Fruits of Solitude*, 1693,1:519).

Sources for quotations

Quotations from the Bible are from the Moffatt translation unless otherwise noted: *A New Translation of the Bible,* by James Moffatt, New York, Harper and Brothers, 1954. Appreciation is expressed to Harper and Row for permission to make use of the quotations. Quotations from the King James Version of the Bible are identified by the initials KJV.

Identified in the notes are the manuscript sources from which quotations by George Fox, Isaac Penington, John Woolman, and other early Quakers are taken. Punctuation and spelling have been modernized.

Quotations from Hasidic stories and sayings and from Martin Buber are taken from books whose titles are abbreviated in the notes as follows: *Tales:* reprinted by permission of Schocken Books, Inc. from *Tales of the Hasidim; Early Masters* by Martin Buber. Copyright ©1947 by Schocken Books, Inc. Copyright ©renewed 1975 by Schocken Books, Inc. *Hasidism: Hasidism* by Martin Buber, New York, Philosophical Library, 1948. *The Way of Man: The Way of Man, according to the Teachings of Hasidism* by Martin Buber, Pendle Hills Pamphlets No. 106, by permission of Routledge and Kegan Paul, London, 1950. *Two Types: Two Types of Faith* by Martin Buber, New York, The Macmillan Company, 1951. *Between Man and Man: Between Man and Man* by Martin Buber, New York, The Macmillan Company, 1949. Appreciation for permission to make use of the quotations is expressed to the respective publishers.

The quotation from Lin Yutang in the note to Chapter 13 is from *The Wisdom of Laotse,* by Lin Yutang, New York, Random House, 1948. Appreciation is expressed to Random House for permission to make use of the quotation.

The quotation from Martin Buber on page 4 is from his 1928 address, "China and Us," included in *Pointing the Way: Collected Essays* by Martin Buber, Harper and Brothers, New York, 1957. Appreciation is expressed to Harper and Row for permission to make use of the quotation.

A KEY TO THE CHAPTERS

First Lines by Number

108